Step Away

The Keys to Resilient Parenting

Kate K. Lund, Psy. D.

© 2025 2MARKET MEDIA

All rights reserved. No portion of this book may be reproduced, stored in a retrieval system, or transmitted in any form or by any means - electronic, mechanical, photocopy, recording, scanning, or other - except for brief quotations in critical reviews or articles, without the prior written permission of the publisher.

The purpose of this book is to educate the reader and encourage broad thinking about the ideas presented in the book. This book is not intended to be a substitute for the advice of a licensed mental health practitioner or certified professional coach. You should always seek professional advice about your specific situation as needed.

Published by 2MARKET MEDIA with Kate K. Lund, Psy. D.

ISBN: 978-0-9971516-4-0

Dedication

To Ted, William, Brady, Squirt and Wally

CONTENTS

Dedication iii

Endorsements vii

Foreword by Jamie Hess xi

Acknowledgments xiii

Introduction: Parents Need Resilience 1

Chapter 1: Why Do You Need to Step Away? 13

Chapter 2: The Elusive Balance of Parenthood 25

Chapter 3: Navigating Stress Day-to-Day 35

Chapter 4: What Is a Resilient Mindset? 47

Chapter 5: Challenges Are Everywhere 57

Chapter 6: Emotionally Intelligent Parenting 67

Chapter 7: Building Resilience Is a Process 77

Chapter 8: Celebrating Your Own Unique Context 87

Chapter 9: Putting Resilience into Practice 97

Chapter 10: Why, How, and When to Seek Help..................................105

Chapter 11: Reflecting on Your Parenting Journey 113

Chapter 12: Living the Keys to Resilient Parenting 121

Chapter 13: Navigating the Uncharted – Resilience in Transition.......129

Chapter 14: The Legacy of Resilience – Building a Future Together....137

FURTHER READING... 143

Endorsements

From sleepless nights with a newborn to the helpless feeling of toddler tantrums, who knew parenting would be so daunting? If you feel unprepared or ill-equipped to handle the endless challenges of parenthood, fear not! With a background in clinical psychology and the mother of twins, Kate Lund knows first-hand what it's like. In *Step Away: The Keys to Resilient Parenting*, she delivers a compelling blueprint to support effective parenting. Powerfully written with compassion and candor, Kate offers a unique perspective to inform, guide, and inspire you to become the kind of parent you always dreamed of. *Step Away* is a timeless tool kit to face parental challenges head-on and to raise your children from infancy to adulthood joyfully.

— **Chuck Garcia, Columbia University Professor and author** *of A Climb to the TOP* **and** *The MOMENT THAT DEFINES YOUR LIFE.*

"As a parent and a leader in transformational work, I deeply appreciate the wisdom and practicality that Dr. Kate Lund brings to *Step Away: The Keys to Resilient Parenting*. Modern parenting is undoubtedly challenging, but Lund provides a powerful and accessible roadmap for resilience—not just for our children, but for us as parents. Her insights into self-care, emotional intelligence, and building strong support networks are invaluable tools for navigating the inevitable stresses of raising children. With her deep expertise as a clinical psychologist and personal experience overcoming adversity, Lund reminds us that resilience is a skill we can cultivate. This book is a must-read for any parent looking to create a healthier, more fulfilling family life while maintaining their own well-being."

— Josselyne Herman-Saccio, Master Coach

"Dr. Kate Lund's book gives parents the permission they deserve to pause, stumble, and reflect—an often overlooked but deeply impactful part of navigating parenthood. With trusted guidance, relatable stories, and a warm, compassionate tone, she offers a reassuring companion for the parenting journey."

— Katie Taylor, CCLS and Founder, Child Life On Call

In a time when parenting feels more overwhelming than ever, Step Away arrives as both a lifeline and a breath of fresh air. Dr. Kate Lund blends clinical expertise with heartfelt personal insight to offer parents a deeply compassionate and practical guide to resilience. What makes this book so powerful is its emphasis on real, actionable steps—rooted in self-care, emotional intelligence, and authentic connection—that empower parents to thrive, not just survive.

Kate's wisdom shines through every page, making it clear that resilience isn't something you're born with—it's something you build. This book is a must-read for any parent who wants to feel more grounded, supported, and hopeful in the midst of daily challenges.

— Place Wilson, Author and Entrepreneur

Endorsements

Dr. Kate Lund brings both deep clinical expertise and personal insight to *Step Away: The Keys to Resilient Parenting*, offering a powerful framework for cultivating resilience in the face of modern parenting challenges. I had the privilege of attending graduate school with Dr. Lund and have long admired her thoughtful, compassionate approach. As a child psychologist with over two decades of experience at Boston Children's Hospital and Harvard Medical School and a mother of four, I found this book to be both timely and essential. Dr. Lund reminds us that resilience is not a fixed trait but a set of skills that can be developed—with lasting benefits for both parents and children. This is a must-read for any parent striving to navigate family life with intention and emotional strength.

— Jennifer Gentile, Child Psychologist

Foreword by Jamie Hess

As a wellness entrepreneur, mom, and advocate for empowered living, I've come to understand that resilience isn't something we simply teach our children—it's something we *model* through every challenge, boundary, and breakthrough. In *Step Away: The Keys to Resilient Parenting*, Dr. Kate Lund brings us a guide that is both deeply personal and profoundly practical. Her words don't just offer insight—they offer a way forward.

Parenting in today's world is no small task. The pressure to get it "right" can feel overwhelming, especially when we're balancing the many roles we play. What Dr. Lund does so brilliantly is invite us to step away from perfectionism and into presence. She offers strategies rooted in science and storytelling, helping parents create space—for themselves and for their kids. Because resilient parenting begins with a regulated parent.

This book reminds us that every difficult moment is an opportunity to build something stronger, more grounded, and more connected. Whether you're navigating tantrums, teens, or your own emotional triggers, you'll find tools in these pages that inspire clarity, calm, and compassion.

Dr. Lund's approach is exactly what we need right now—empathetic, empowering, and actionable. I'm honored to share this journey with you and invite you to embrace *Step Away*, not just as a parenting manual but as a mindset. Let this book support you in showing up, not as a perfect parent but as a resilient one.

— *Jamie Hess, mom and mindset coach*

Acknowledgments

Writing *Step Away: The Keys to Resilient Parenting* has been a deeply personal and transformative journey—one that would not have been possible without the support, guidance, and encouragement of so many incredible people.

To my family—thank you for being my anchor, my inspiration, and my greatest teachers. Your patience, love, and belief in me made this book possible.

To the team at 2MM—your vision, expertise, and dedication helped bring this project to life. Thank you.

A heartfelt thank-you to my editors, Brenda Newmann and Greg Likins, for your thoughtful insights, careful attention to detail, and unwavering commitment to the integrity of this work. Your editorial guidance was invaluable.

And to the countless friends, colleagues, and supporters who have encouraged me, offered feedback, or simply believed in the message of this book—thank you. Your presence and enthusiasm have meant the world.

This book is a testament to the power of resilience, community, and shared growth. I am truly grateful to walk this path with all of you.

INTRODUCTION

Parents Need Resilience

Parenting brings joy, wonder, and excitement, yet the demands of modern parenting can also test our limits, unlike anything else. As a clinical psychologist, I regularly encounter parents struggling under relentless physical and mental pressure; as a mother of seventeen-year-old twin boys, I'm no stranger to the stress, exhaustion, and burnout that so often result from the challenges of parenting. That's where this book comes in. By applying research-based principles, you can build resilience, manage stress, and become better equipped to maximize your potential as a parent.

Resilient parenting is an approach that involves integrating ideas and practices that strengthen your ability to navigate the inevitable difficulties of parenthood. Resilient parenting doesn't promote pushing through at the expense of your health and well-being. Instead, it emphasizes the importance of practicing self-care, utilizing problem-solving skills, and exercising emotional intelligence. It's about resisting the temptation to intervene every time a problem arises and leaning on your support network so that you and your children can flourish. Resilient parents accept that parenting is challenging and that they are doing their best given their unique circumstances. By practicing resilience, they are modeling vital skills for their children and equipping them with the tools to navigate life's challenges.

This book combines over twenty years of experience in clinical psychology, working with children, parents, and athletes, along with the latest research on resilience. The study of resilience has evolved significantly in recent decades, shifting from simply understanding how we manage challenges to a more comprehensive understanding of the internal and external factors that enhance our ability to cope under pressure.

Resilience therapy has evolved into an integrative approach, which draws on evidence-based therapies (i.e., cognitive behavioral therapy [CBT], acceptance and commitment therapy [ACT], and narrative therapy) and focuses on mental flexibility, emotional regulation, and problem-solving skills, crucial components for fostering a healthy, supportive family environment. Unlike other therapeutic approaches that focus on diagnosing and treating mental health issues, resilience therapy focuses on strengths, adaptive functioning, and one's long-term capacity for thriving.

In this book, you'll find a framework for resilient parenting, a tool kit of techniques and approaches that you can apply to the unique challenges parenting presents. While there's no one-size-fits-all in parenting, all parents will face challenges; it's how you respond and grow through those challenges that is most important. Every parent has their baseline level of coping, with unique strengths and weaknesses. Some may be knocked down more easily than others, and that's okay. What matters most is having the tools to manage those challenges. Developing resilience can help you become a more relaxed, happy, and empathetic parent, benefiting both you and your children.

The Power of Resilience: My Story

Resilience has always been important to me. When I was four years old, I was diagnosed with hydrocephalus, a complex medical condition that required numerous surgeries, nights in the hospital, and prolonged periods of recovery. I would frequently return to school looking and feeling different from other kids. I missed out on a lot, which added to the challenge. There were many things I couldn't do, and sometimes I had to learn that the hard way.

I remember being twelve years old and watching as all the other children played on a trampoline at a friend's birthday party. I wanted so badly to join in, and the desire to be part of that moment pushed me to ignore the many warnings I had internalized from my parents and doctors. For a moment, bouncing up and down was wonderful, until it wasn't. My head started to spin so much that I had to leave the party, and I felt dizzy for a week. Children often need to learn from experience to truly appreciate what they have been told. For me, moments like these were powerful learning experiences. I would always have to adapt to unique challenges and learn to appreciate my circumstances, along with the challenges and opportunities they presented. With the support of parents, friends, and family, I learned to love the sports I could play, even if I was never going to be the best at them. I found ways to manage my condition so I could get the best out of my education and enjoy many of the same experiences my peers did. I came to see the value in the challenges I faced, the opportunities for growth they provided, and the possibility of a positive outcome on the other side.

I've always been aware of how my early foundation in resilience helped me through numerous challenges, but it wasn't until I became a psychologist that I started to look at resilience more closely. In my mid-twenties, I left a career in public relations in Washington, DC, to return to school and pursue my long-term goal of working in clinical psychology. I got accepted to a doctoral program at William James College (formerly The Massachusetts School of Professional Psychology)., and during my time there, I spent four years doing fieldwork at hospitals associated with Harvard Medical School. For two of those years, I worked with children and their families at the Shriners Hospital for Children in Boston.

Working so closely with young children, many of whom were being treated for serious burn injuries, brought back memories of my childhood, and I was once again struck by the power of resilience. I knew the children at Shriners were getting the best medical care possible, but as a psychologist, my role was to help them build both internal and external resources to manage their recoveries. I aimed to help them understand their injuries and create a new sense of normal. I also helped the kids and families I worked with to see the possibilities beyond the challenges they faced.

While working at Shriners, I also witnessed the heavy psychological toll that a child's serious, sometimes life-threatening injury could take on parents. They grapple with intense worry while having to adjust their lives and their entire approach to parenthood. I was struck by the resilience of my parents back when I was hospitalized. Their calm presence and support helped me through so many challenges when I was young. They helped me to accept my reality and encouraged me to recognize and appreciate the things I could do and not just focus on the things I couldn't do. This made me realize that resilience operates on both an individual and social level, and that resilient parents play a crucial role in modeling those qualities for their children.

During this period, I began exploring the concept of resilience more deeply. I was particularly interested in studies that focused on recovery from medical illness and injury. Many of these studies highlighted the crucial role of robust psychological and social support systems, and interventions to manage pain and help children visualize the possibility of recovery. Remarkably, these studies revealed that many children not only heal but often experience post-traumatic growth, emerging with a stronger sense of self, improved coping skills, and, in some cases, a new outlook on life. Researchers like David Chedekel, EdD, and Frederick Stoddard, MD, have extensively studied the long-term psychological impact of burn injuries on children. Their work highlights the value of psychological support and interventions in aiding both medical treatment and long-term psychological recovery.

The work of Chedekel and Stoddard inspired my doctoral research project focusing on the effects of pressure garment therapy on young burn patients. This therapy is imperative in the wound healing process, but wearing tight-fitting garments for extended periods can also be incredibly painful. In my research, I saw how parental and family support were vital for boosting the overall resilience of young patients, helping them to endure painful treatments. I also observed how interventions like drama and music therapy could help children manage pain and tolerate the unpleasant aspects of recovery. I saw the work parents had to do to maintain their resilient mindset, often putting their feelings aside to remain calm and reassuring during treatments and help children to understand the long-term benefits that could come from temporary pain and discomfort.

After I completed my doctoral research, my husband and I moved to Connecticut, and I started working as a psychologist at the University of Hartford. I provided therapy to students and athletes dealing with the many social, academic, and physical challenges related to university life. It was here that I started thinking about how to incorporate ideas related to resilience more fully into my clinical practice. Research showed that resilience is rooted in key psychological and behavioral traits such as flexibility, emotional regulation, growth mindset, and the ability to both give and receive social support. The research confirmed what I had always believed: that resilience isn't a fixed trait. It can be nurtured by implementing behavioral and psychological strategies designed to make us more resilient and increase our capacity to handle adversity. These strategies and interventions, such as gratitude journaling, self-care, stress management, visualization, cognitive reframing, and mindfulness, were at the core of one's ability to overcome serious adversity like medical illness, but also in empowering individuals to navigate daily challenges, maintain emotional balance, and thrive within the context of their lives.

I started thinking about how to apply the research on resilience to the everyday lives of children and wrote my first book, *Bounce: Help Your Child Build Resilience and Thrive in School, Sports, and Life*.

Bounce outlined seven pillars of raising resilient children:

- Managing emotion and tolerating frustration
- Navigating friendship and social pressure
- Sustaining focus and attention
- Developing courage
- Building motivation
- Finding confidence
- Creating optimism

I've used these pillars to help parents guide their children through a range of developmental challenges, such as struggling with schoolwork, behavior, physical and mental health, body image, sports, addiction, or any of the myriad other difficulties children face. I've also been able to apply this model of resilience to my other passion, working with athletes to help them optimize their performance.

In recent years, my practice has shifted to working more with adults, many of whom are parents struggling to balance the demands of parenthood alongside their careers and countless other responsibilities. It's something I can certainly relate to. When our children were very young, my husband traveled most days of the week for work. I often felt like I was continuously fighting fires, bouncing from one challenge to the next with little time to plan and think about my interests alongside those of our children. What I came to realize, through my own lived experience as well as working with hundreds of parents, is that nurturing resilience in yourself as a parent and nurturing resilience in your children are often two sides of the same coin. Parents often get mired in the immediate challenges of life and lose sight of the bigger picture. We forget that if we can help ourselves develop a resilient mindset, we can help our children to do the same.

That parents need resilience is unavoidable. Substantial evidence indicates that parenting is more challenging than ever. A 2023 study by the American Psychological Association revealed that 48 percent of parents regularly feel completely overwhelmed by stress. This alarming reality prompted US Surgeon General Vivek Murthy to issue an advisory highlighting the importance of parental mental health and well-being, stressing that we cannot effectively address the mental health crisis affecting young children without also implementing strategies to support the mental health and well-being of parents.

It All Starts with Stepping Away

The first thing I teach parents about resilient parenting is the idea of stepping away. Stepping away is a practice of self-care that creates space mentally, emotionally, and physically in our hectic lives and calms the central nervous system. In practice, it can take many forms, such as a two-minute breather, regular exercise, or engaging in hobbies and social activities. The goal of stepping away is to create space between ourselves and our parenting, allowing us to approach challenges more effectively and with a greater sense of calm. As parents, we love our children and we'd do anything for them, but the reality is that not all challenges are emergencies. Stepping away in the face of a nonemergency challenge protects parental well-being and is vital for preserving the perspective, clarity, and emotional intelligence required to guide children through their early lives. Stepping away is not about disengaging; it is about choosing a more grounded response that supports resilience in both parents and children.

I'll explore this simple yet essential skill throughout this book. There are no hard-and-fast rules; instead, I aim to provide you with a framework for why, how, and when to step away. While the intensity and degree of challenges will vary, resilient parents can strike a balance between when to intervene, when to guide a child through a challenge, and when to step back and let a child grapple with problems on their own. The principles outlined in this book serve as a guide for finding this balance. I will show you how being conscious and deliberate in your approach to self-care and nonintervention can form the foundation of resilient parenting, improving the well-being of the entire family and creating an environment of clarity, calm, and ease.

This book is filled with examples of parents who have made significant changes in their lives, enabling them to become more resilient and better equipped to overcome the challenges their families face. These examples are based on my clinical experience and research. However, to protect client confidentiality, none of the names are real, and no story represents a single individual. Instead, they are composite narratives that combine elements from various real-life cases, ensuring anonymity while still reflecting the authentic human experiences I see in my work.

Aisha's Story: Stepping Away to Rediscover Lost Passions

One of my clients found herself in a situation that many of us can relate to. As a fifty-two-year-old woman, she came to me suffering from extreme stress, mood-related symptoms, anxiety, and dissatisfaction with her weight. Before becoming a parent, she had been a serious triathlete, but life as a working mom had made it difficult to maintain her training regimen, and by the time we met, she had all but put her competitive ambitions behind her.

The first thing we worked on was the idea of stepping away in the moment. My client was struggling to control her emotions and would frequently suffer panic attacks in the face of challenging situations. We worked together to identify common challenges and triggers, along with a range of strategies for approaching them. She found deep breathing to be a useful tool for calming the central nervous system before taking two minutes to put the situation into context and plan how she would deal with a problem without letting her emotions escalate to the point of shutdown.

As part of our coaching, I worked with my client to take a closer look at herself and the personal goals that she had lost sight of. She reconnected with her triathlon coach and found ways to integrate training and physical recovery into her daily routine. With this newfound confidence, she went on to compete again. It was a huge win that transformed her life in many ways. Reducing her stress meant she was more emotionally available for her family, and her relationship with her kids improved. She rediscovered her confidence along with the resilient mindset needed to navigate parenting challenges and manage stress.

Aisha was surprised to discover that stepping away to focus on her ambitions gave her children space to do the same. Her eldest daughter struggled with insecurities about her fitness and body image that had put her off exercising and participating in sports. Seeing her mother change her approach to exercise inspired her to do the same; she went back to playing field hockey, a sport she had enjoyed when she was younger. Instead of trying to solve her daughter's problems, Aisha led by example, showing her how to cultivate courage, take action, and feel more fulfilled.

When you pick up this book, I want you to feel hopeful. The emotional and physical toll of modern parenting is real, and if you're feeling it, you're not alone. You're also not alone in seeking strategies to manage it. The first challenge is to step away, look inward, and recognize the things that are important to you. Then, find ways of integrating them into your life, even if you can't make them your priority. I want to help readers reframe the idea that by practicing self-care, parents are somehow being selfish. The opposite is true; when you learn how to care for yourself, manage stress, and adopt a resilient mindset, you are far better equipped to support your children through all the challenges, big and small, that they will face. The goal of this process is to find more purpose, joy, and clarity, so you can become the best version of yourself, for the sake of you, your children, and your family.

CHAPTER 1

Why Do You Need to Step Away?

When our twin boys were infants, my husband's job took him across the country for weeks at a time, leaving me to navigate the whirlwind of parenthood alone. As a clinical psychologist, I thought I was equipped to handle stress, but nothing prepared me for the relentless demands of raising two babies while juggling household chores, my career, and my own well-being. Imagine the scene: one boy screaming for a bottle, the other spitting up on my last clean shirt, the phone buzzing with work emails, and a sink full of dishes staring me down. Every parent knows this chaos: sleepless nights, teething tantrums, potty-training disasters, and the constant juggle of feeding, soothing, and creating a nurturing environment where kids can play, learn, and grow.

In those early years, I let my own needs slide. I'd skip breakfast, trade workouts for extra laundry loads, and push through exhaustion to keep the family afloat. I told myself I was doing it for our boys, but the harder I pushed, the more stress piled up. I was running on fumes, and it showed, snapping over small spills, feeling guilty for not being "present" enough, and losing the energy to enjoy my kids. The breaking point came when I caught a sinus infection from one of the boys. It wasn't just a cold; it knocked me down for weeks. I could barely lift my head off the pillow, my head throbbing, my body aching. I'd never been so knocked out by a simple virus. That was my wake-up call: I couldn't keep neglecting myself and expect to be the parent our boys needed.

I started small, committing to one apple a day and a walk to boost my overall well-being. It wasn't much, but it was a tangible step. I permitted myself to rest, taking short walks around the block, breathing in the crisp air, and reflecting on my parenting load. I journaled about what was working, what wasn't, and what I needed to feel whole again. Slowly, I felt my energy return. My mind cleared, and I started to see things differently. Not every meltdown was an emergency. When I was sick, my family managed better than I expected: The boys played together, my parents stepped in, and the world didn't fall apart. This realization hit hard: Stepping away wasn't a luxury; it was a necessity.

Those moments of stepping away, whether a walk, a quiet coffee, or a chat with a friend, recharged me. I started exercising again, even if it was just a fifteen-minute yoga flow. I carved out time to read novels, not just professional books, and reconnected with friends over brunch. These weren't selfish acts; they made me a better parent. I was more patient, more empathetic, and more present with our boys. I could laugh at their silly antics instead of stressing over the mess they made. As a psychologist, I've seen this pattern in countless parents: When you prioritize yourself, you show up stronger for your kids.

Stepping away didn't just help me; it shaped our boys' resilience too. By taking time to recharge, I modeled how to handle stress and emotions, teaching them skills to navigate life's challenges. They saw me pause before reacting, breathe through frustration, and come back ready to listen. Over time, I noticed them mimicking these habits, taking a moment to calm down during a sibling spat or asking for a break when homework felt overwhelming. As a clinician, I've used this approach to help families build what I call resilient parenting, a set of habits that keep you steady while guiding your kids to thrive.

Resilient parenting isn't about powering through every challenge; it's about building habits that sustain you and your family. It's about modeling the skills your kids need to face life's ups and downs. Here are the key traits of resilient parents, which we'll explore throughout this book:

Trait	What It Means
Flexibility	Adapting your parenting as your kids grow and life changes.
Stress Management	Spotting stress in yourself and your kids and handling it with calm strategies.
Self-Awareness	Knowing your strengths and limits, focusing on your family's unique needs.
Problem-Solving	Turning challenges into chances for you and your kids to learn and grow.
Social Support	Leaning on friends, family, or community for help when things get tough.

Trait	What It Means
Resilient Mindset	Seeing challenges as opportunities to grow, not as roadblocks.
Emotional Intelligence	Staying in tune with your and your kids' emotions, fostering empathy and connection.
Effective Communication	Listening actively and explaining choices to build trust with your kids.
Boundaries and Independence	Setting healthy limits while encouraging kids to explore, fail, and grow.

These traits aren't out of reach; you likely already practice many of them. This book will help you strengthen them, starting with one core strategy: stepping away. This simple act can transform how you parent and how your kids develop, and it's a tool I've seen work wonders in my own life and with the families I counsel.

Laura's Story: Stepping Away in the Moment

Laura, a single mom of two, came home after a long day at her office job to find her eleven-year-old son, Marcus, slumped over his math homework. Their house rule was firm: homework before TV. But Marcus was struggling with fractions, a new concept that left him frustrated and ready to quit. He told Laura he'd had enough and wanted to watch his favorite show. Their conversation started to heat up, Marcus's voice rising, Laura's patience thinning. Her instinct was to dive in and solve the problem, easing his stress and her own. But she was exhausted from work, her head still buzzing with emails and deadlines, and she knew her frustration could spark a bigger conflict.

Instead of pushing through, Laura paused. She took a deep breath and told Marcus they'd tackle the homework in ten minutes. She suggested he grab a snack or a glass of water while she stepped into her bedroom. There, she changed out of her work clothes, sat on the edge of her bed, and practiced a quick breathing exercise: three deep inhales, three slow exhales. This brief pause helped her shift from stressed-out employee to supportive mom. She reminded herself that Marcus wasn't just fighting math; he was learning how to handle challenges.

When Laura returned, she felt calmer, clearer. Instead of giving Marcus the answers, she sat beside him and asked guiding questions: "What part feels tricky? Can you explain what you tried?" Her tone was patient, not rushed. Together, they worked through the problem, and Marcus lit up when he finally got it. After they finished, Laura shared a simple lesson: "Sometimes, when things feel overwhelming, a short break can help you think clearly. You can try it next time math feels hard or even with a friend." Marcus nodded, and Laura saw a spark of understanding; he'd learned a strategy for life, not just homework.

Laura's pause did more than defuse the moment. It modeled self-regulation and problem-solving. Studies show that frequent yelling or overreacting can stress kids out, lowering their confidence and straining the parent–child bond. By stepping away, Laura avoided an outburst, kept their connection strong, and showed

Marcus how to manage frustration. She also gave him space to wrestle with the problem, fostering his independence and confidence.

The Benefits of Stepping Away

Stepping away is a powerful tool with benefits that ripple through your family. Here's how it helps:

- **Gaining perspective**: When you're caught in a tense moment, like a homework battle or a toddler tantrum, it's easy to lose sight of the bigger picture. Stepping away lets you zoom out. For Laura, it meant focusing on Marcus's growth, not just getting the homework done. A five-minute pause can shift your mindset from reactive to thoughtful.

- **Managing emotions**: Parenting stirs up a roller coaster of feelings: love, joy, frustration, and even anger. A brief break helps you regulate those emotions, keeping you calm and present. Research shows that parents who manage their emotions avoid outbursts that can stress kids out, preserving trust and connection.

- **Avoiding burnout**: Parenting is relentless, and burnout is a real risk. Studies highlight that parents who prioritize self-care, like short breaks, exercise, or time with friends, feel less overwhelmed and build stronger relationships with their kids. For Laura, a few minutes alone was enough to recharge, letting her return with patience and energy.

- **Encouraging independence**: When you step back, kids get space to solve problems. Laura's questions helped Marcus learn, not just follow instructions. This builds confidence and resilience, teaching kids they can handle challenges on their own.

- **Strengthening bonds**: Time away makes you more patient and attentive, deepening your connection with your kids. Laura's calm approach made Marcus feel supported, not pressured, fostering a stronger bond.

- **Modeling boundaries**: By showing kids you have needs, you teach them to respect boundaries, a skill they'll need for friendships, school, and beyond. Laura's pause showed Marcus that taking a break is okay, even for grown-ups.

Melanie's Story: Stepping Away for Balance

Melanie, a mom of a four-year-old daughter and a seven-year-old son, came to my practice feeling like she was drowning. Her high-pressure job as a marketing manager, combined with parenting two young kids, left her exhausted and short-tempered. She'd snap at her kids over small things, like spilled juice or a forgotten toy, then feel crushed by guilt. To cope, she stayed up late, tackling work emails and chores, but it only made her more irritable and disconnected from her family. Her home, once a place of warmth, started to feel tense and chaotic.

When I suggested stepping away, Melanie was skeptical. She worried it would mean neglecting her kids or letting tasks pile up. She feared that taking time for herself would make her feel even more behind. But as we talked, we explored what brought her joy before parenthood: yoga; quiet moments with her husband, Sam; and catching up with friends over coffee. These weren't just hobbies; they were lifelines to her sense of self. We built a plan to weave them into her routine, starting small to make it manageable.

Melanie and Sam agreed she'd take thirty minutes after dinner for yoga while the kids played or read quietly. At first, Melanie worried the kids would feel ignored, but they adapted faster than she expected. Her daughter started "reading" picture books to her stuffed animals, and her son dove into his chapter books. Sam used the time to read or catch up on a podcast, and soon the whole family looked forward to this calm window. Bedtime, once a nightly battle of whining and stalling, became smoother and even joyful. The kids were more relaxed, and Melanie felt like she could breathe again.

Melanie also started taking five-minute breaks during tough moments. When a sibling argument erupted or her daughter refused to put on her shoes, she'd step into the kitchen, close her eyes, and take slow, deep breaths. She explained to her kids in simple terms, "Mommy needs a quick time-out to feel calm, just like you do sometimes." This honesty helped them understand, and soon they were asking for their own "time-outs" when they felt overwhelmed. Melanie noticed she was more patient, and her clearer head helped her tackle parenting challenges, like negotiating a truce between her kids, with creative solutions.

Over time, Melanie made bigger changes. She and Sam hired a babysitter once a month for a date night, rekindling their connection over dinner or a movie. They teamed up with friends to share after-school childcare, giving Melanie time to catch up on work or meet a friend for coffee. She explained these changes to her kids, saying, "Mommy and Daddy need time to feel happy so we can be the best parents for you." The kids began to respect her boundaries, and Melanie noticed them mimicking her habits, like taking a deep breath before reacting or asking for space during a tough moment.

Melanie's story shows how stepping away can transform a family. It wasn't about abandoning her responsibilities; it was about reclaiming her energy to be a more effective, loving parent. Research supports this: Parents who practice self-care and set boundaries have better well-being and stronger relationships with their kids. Melanie's kids learned to regulate their emotions and respect others' needs, building resilience that will serve them for life.

Stepping Away in Everyday Life

Stepping away doesn't always mean big changes. It can be as simple as pausing to breathe when a tantrum hits, taking a walk around the block, or savoring a quiet coffee before the kids wake up. For me, it was those early morning walks when the twins were napping, feeling the sun on my face, and letting my mind wander. For Laura, it was a few minutes in her bedroom to reset. For Melanie, it was yoga and date nights. The key is finding what works for you, something that recharges your body and mind.

This strategy also teaches kids that it's okay to have needs. When my boys saw me take a break to read or call a friend, they learned that parents aren't superheroes who never tire. They started to understand boundaries, like when I said, "Mommy needs ten minutes to finish this, then we'll play." Over time, they began asking for their own space, like time to draw or play alone, which built their independence and confidence.

As a psychologist, I've seen parents step away from work in all kinds of ways. One client, a dad of three, started running during his lunch break to clear his head. Another, a mom of a toddler, took five minutes each evening to listen to music and dance in her kitchen. These small acts didn't just help them cope; they made them more present and patient with their kids. Studies back this up: Parents who carve out time for themselves feel less burned out and build stronger, more trusting relationships with their children.

Why Stepping Away Matters

Stepping away isn't about checking out of parenting; it's about showing up as your best self. It's a strategy to manage stress, model resilience, and foster independence in your kids. Whether it's a quick pause to breathe, a daily workout, or a night out with friends, these moments recharge you and strengthen your family. They show your kids how to handle life's challenges with calm and confidence, setting them up to become resilient adults.

This chapter has explored how stepping away builds resilience for you and your kids. It's not just about surviving parenthood; it's about thriving in it. As we move forward, we'll dive deeper into the traits of resilient parenting, exploring how to balance involvement with independence. How do you know when to step in and when to let go? What small shifts can create positive change for you and your kids? The next chapter explores practical ways to navigate the challenges of parenthood with more clarity and confidence.

CHAPTER 2

The Elusive Balance of Parenthood

Parenting can flip your world upside down. Before our twins arrived, friends and family warned me that life would change, and I nodded along, thinking I was ready. I pictured myself juggling a thriving career as a clinical psychologist, staying fit, keeping a tidy home, and being the kind of mom who bakes cookies and reads bedtime stories with endless patience. But when the boys were born, reality hit hard: sleepless nights, diaper disasters, and a to-do list that grew faster than I could keep up. I clung to this image of "having it all," a balanced life where every piece fit perfectly. Spoiler alert: It didn't.

It took years to accept that perfect balance is a myth. Parenting isn't about nailing every role—caregiver, professional, partner, friend—every day. It's about adapting, forgiving yourself when things don't go as planned, and focusing on what matters most in the moment. Resilient parenting, as I've learned through my journey and years of working with families, is about embracing the messiness. It's about showing up for your kids with compassion and flexibility, even when you're not at your best. You don't need to be a superhero; you just need to be responsive.

Diego's Story: Choosing What Matters Most

Let's talk about Diego, a single dad whose chaotic weekend taught him a powerful lesson about resilience. Diego always imagined that parenting his six-year-old daughter, Laila, would mean structured, joyful days, pancake breakfasts, park adventures, and cozy story times. But real life? It was messier. One Saturday, Diego woke up already swamped with work emails and a pile of laundry. He planned to kick off the day with homemade pancakes, a special treat for Laila. But Laila had other ideas. By 7 a.m., she'd turned the living room into a superhero obstacle course, zooming around with her stuffed animals in tow.

Diego tried to keep up, joining her "rescue missions" while glancing at the clock. They were already running late for Laila's soccer practice. Breakfast became a rushed bowl of cereal, spilled twice in the chaos, and they dashed out, only to turn back five minutes later for her forgotten cleats. At practice, while other parents chatted, Diego hunched over his laptop, trying to catch up on work. Every few minutes, he looked up to cheer for Laila, but guilt gnawed at him. He wasn't fully present for her, and his inbox was still overflowing.

Back home, Diego juggled laundry, meal prep, and playing with Laila, but every task felt half done. By evening, both were cranky. Their story time was short and tense, with Laila fidgeting and Diego's mind elsewhere. As he tucked her in, he felt defeated. The house was a mess, his work was unfinished, and he hadn't connected with Laila the way he'd hoped. He wondered how he'd gotten it so wrong.

That night, Diego made a promise to himself: the next day would be different. He asked a simple question: *What's my priority right now?* The answer was clear: quality time with Laila. The next morning, they left their phones and chores behind and went for a walk. That walk turned into a picnic, then a tree-climbing adventure in the park. Laila's laughter filled the air as they hunted for the "best" climbing tree. They came home exhausted but happy, their bond stronger than ever. Work and chores could wait until Monday. Diego realized that harmony wasn't about doing everything; it was about choosing what mattered most and letting go of the rest.

Diego's shift in perspective was a game changer. Some weekends, he might need to prioritize work or ask another parent to take Laila to soccer. Other times, like that Sunday, Laila came first. By staying flexible and forgiving himself for an imperfect house or inbox, Diego built resilience, not just for himself, but for Laila, who learned that love and presence matter more than a perfect plan.

The Demands on Modern Parents

Diego's story resonates because parenting today feels like juggling five full-time jobs. You're a caregiver, a professional, a partner, a friend, and often a volunteer or team parent, all while keeping up with soccer practices and school projects. Society expects you to nail every role without breaking a sweat. But let's be real: It's exhausting, and the pressure to "do it all" can leave you feeling like you're failing.

When we moved to Boston, my husband and I were 200 miles from family. With him traveling for work, I was often on my own with the twins. I tried to handle everything—parenting, work, and housework—without asking for help. It wasn't sustainable. Hiring a part-time nanny was a lifeline, giving me space to breathe and focus on my career. I also joined a local moms' group, where I found not just support but real friendship for me and playmates for our boys. These connections reminded me that leaning on others isn't a weakness; it's a cornerstone of resilient parenting.

Then there's the social pressure. Scroll through social media, and you're bombarded with images of perfect families: kids acing every activity, homes straight out of a design magazine, parents running marathons and posting about their latest vacation. It's easy to feel inadequate. In my practice, I see parents who beat themselves up for not keeping up with chores, fitness goals, or their kids' extracurriculars. A 2014 study in *Psychology of Popular Media Culture* found that spending too much time online, especially comparing yourself to others, can impact your self-esteem. Those "perfect" posts? They're curated, not real life. No one's house is spotless 24/7, and no parent has it all together.

The first step to resilience is letting go of those unrealistic ideals. Every family is different, and your challenges are real. Maybe you're a single parent like Diego, or maybe you're balancing a demanding job and a toddler's tantrums. Recognizing your unique situation helps you set realistic goals and be kinder to yourself. It's not about being perfect; it's about doing your best with what you have.

Understanding Your Context

Before we dive into strategies, let's talk about why balance feels so hard. In my work as a psychologist, I start by helping parents understand their unique context, the specific pressures shaping their lives. This isn't about judging yourself; it's about seeing your reality clearly so you can focus on what matters. Here's a quick checklist to help you reflect:

- **Family structure**: Every family is unique. Maybe you're a single parent, in a same-sex partnership, or part of a blended family with step kids. You might have grandparents living with you or friends who pitch in. Understanding your setup helps you spot your strengths and challenges.

- **Cultural context**: Your culture shapes how you parent, expectations around discipline, family roles, or even holiday traditions. Navigating these norms can affect how you juggle work, family, and personal time.

- **Support network**: Who's in your corner? Maybe you've got family nearby, or maybe you're building connections through school or community groups. Knowing who you can lean on is key.

- **Work schedule**: Work often spills into family life. Long hours, travel, or inflexible bosses can make parenting feel like a marathon. Acknowledge how your job impacts your time and energy.

- **Developmental stages**: A toddler's needs differ from a teen's, and even kids within the same developmental stage need different things. For example, our twins, now 17, are not on the same timeline. They have different strengths and different challenges. This is normal and expected. Avoid comparing your kids to others, even siblings.

- **Finances**: Money worries add stress. Budgeting for childcare, activities, or unexpected expenses can take a toll. Recognizing this helps you plan realistically.

- **Values and goals**: What matters to you? Maybe it's family dinners, outdoor adventures, or reading together. Aligning your time with your values brings a sense of purpose.

Let's see this in action. I worked with a mom, Sarah, who felt overwhelmed raising her two kids while working part-time. Using the checklist, she realized her biggest challenge was her lack of nearby family. She joined a local parenting group, which gave her kids playdates and her a chance to vent with other moms. She also valued creativity but hadn't painted in years. Scheduling one evening a week for art while her partner watched the kids rekindled her spark. Understanding her context helped Sarah focus on what she could control, making parenting feel more joyful.

This checklist isn't just a tool; it's a way to be kinder to yourself. You're not failing when you can't do it all; you're navigating a unique set of demands. By seeing your reality clearly, you can prioritize what matters and let go of what doesn't.

Strategies for Striving Toward Harmony

Now that you've reflected on your context, let's explore ways to manage parenting's demands. I use "strive" because perfect balance is a myth; what matters is finding harmony that works for you. Here are practical strategies to build resilience, with examples to bring them to life:

- **Prioritize**: Figure out what matters most right now. Diego chose Laila over chores one weekend, but another time, he might prioritize work. Make a list of yearly, monthly, and weekly goals. Time-blocking, setting aside specific hours for tasks, helps you stay focused. For example, I block an hour each evening for family time, no phones allowed.

- **Build routines**: Kids thrive on consistency, and routines help you too. A predictable bedtime or dinner schedule creates stability. When our twins were young, our evening routine—dinner, bath, story—gave us all something to count on, even on tough days.

- **Stay flexible**: Life throws curveballs: sick kids, canceled plans, or unexpected work deadlines. Build buffers, like extra time for tasks or a backup childcare plan. When a stomach bug hit our house, I leaned on a neighbor to pick up the boys from school, giving me time to rest and recover.

- **Set boundaries**: Multitasking sounds great, but it often backfires. Checking emails while playing with your kids splits your focus. Set clear lines, like no work after 6 p.m., to be fully present. I stopped answering work calls during dinner, and it made our evenings feel sacred.

- **Focus on quality time**: You don't need hours with your kids, just meaningful moments. A fifteen-minute game or a heartfelt chat can mean more than a distracted day together. Diego's picnic with Laila was short but unforgettable.

- **Practice self-care**: You can't pour from an empty cup. Whether it's a walk, a hobby, or a nap, make time for yourself. I started meditating for twenty minutes a day, and it made a huge difference in my overall sense of well-being.

- **Lean on support**: Friends, family, or community groups can share the load. When I joined a moms' group, I found not just help but lifelong friends. Even small gestures, like a neighbor dropping off dinner, can make a difference.

- **Communicate openly**: Talk to your partner, co-parent, or kids about your needs. When I needed an hour to prep for a work meeting, I told the boys, "Mom needs focus time, then we'll play." They got it, and it taught them to respect boundaries.

These strategies aren't one-size-fits-all. Experiment, adjust, and find what fits your life. Research shows that when you understand why a change matters, like prioritizing self-care for better parenting, you're more likely to stick with it. Support from a therapist, partner, or friend can make the process easier, validating your efforts as you go.

Maya's Story: Building a New Routine

Maya, a high school teacher and mom of two boys, ages seven and ten, who was stretched thin. Her long commute and endless responsibilities—grading papers, cooking, driving to soccer—left her frazzled. Weekends were her chance to catch up, but she often ended up overwhelmed, with no plans for the outdoor adventures she loved. She felt like she was failing her kids, putting them in front of the TV so she could tackle chores or work.

It hit Maya during a parent–teacher conference, where she was the parent, not the teacher. A colleague commented on how "together" she seemed, but inside, Maya was crumbling. Her to-do list was endless, and she was too tired to connect with her boys. She came to me seeking a way to feel less like she was drowning.

We started by exploring what she missed: time outdoors, laughter with her kids, and a sense of calm. Here's how Maya built new habits:

- **Morning ritual**: She woke up twenty minutes early for yoga and a quick planning session, jotting down the day's priorities. It set a calm tone for her hectic schedule.
- **Quality time**: Maya made dinnertime phone-free, focusing on stories and silly debates with her boys. Those thirty minutes became the highlight of their day.
- **Work boundaries**: She stopped answering work emails after 5 p.m., giving her evenings back to her family. It was hard at first, but her colleagues adjusted.
- **Weekend adventures**: Maya and her boys made a bucket list of outdoor activities, including hiking, kite flying,

and stargazing. Saturdays were for exploring, Sundays for relaxing or pursuing individual hobbies.

- **Support network**: She joined a local parent group, trading babysitting with other moms. This gave her time for herself and let her boys build friendships.
- **Self-care**: Maya enrolled in an online creative writing course, carving out Tuesday and Thursday nights for herself. It rekindled a passion she'd forgotten.

These changes didn't happen overnight, but they transformed Maya's life. Her boys were happier, doing better in school, and their home felt lighter. Maya learned that harmony wasn't about perfection; it was about making intentional choices that aligned with her values.

Moving Forward with Resilience

Parenting is a wild, messy journey, and harmony comes from embracing that mess. Diego and Maya found it by letting go of unrealistic ideals and focusing on what mattered most. By understanding your unique context—your family, your challenges, and your values—you can craft strategies that work for you. Resilient parenting isn't about being perfect; it's about responding to life's demands with flexibility and self-compassion. What's one choice that could create meaningful change for your family? In the next chapter, we'll explore how to deepen these strategies and how to use them in a meaningful way.

CHAPTER 3

Navigating Stress Day-to-Day

Parenting can feel like a runaway train. You start the day with a plan—pancakes and a park outing, everyone smiling—only for it to derail by 8 a.m. A simple "put on your shoes" sparks a meltdown, complete with Oscar-worthy floor flopping. The "right" cereal bowl is in the dishwasher, turning breakfast into a negotiation. By the time you're out the door, your peaceful morning is a whirlwind of frayed nerves and raised voices, pushing your patience to the edge.

How you handle these moments depends on where you're at. If you're already exhausted, stressed, or stretched thin, a tantrum can tip you over, leading to a snap you regret. But when you're rested and calm, you're more likely to stay steady, maybe even laugh off the chaos. Most parents know that managing stress makes them better at handling challenges, yet finding time to recharge is a struggle. In this chapter, we'll explore how to build self-care habits that lower your baseline stress, helping you face parenting's wild moments with clarity and calm.

As a clinical psychologist, I start by asking overwhelmed parents: What are you doing to step away? When do you feel most at ease? What makes you forget your to-do list? Most parents are so swamped with tasks—laundry, work, and school runs—they forget to think about what they need to feel good. Stepping away isn't one-size-fits-all. For some, it's meditation or deep breathing to soothe the nervous system. Others find peace in music, a good book, or a quiet moment with tea. Exercise, like running or swimming, works wonders for many, while creative outlets—painting, writing, or DIY projects—can be a lifeline. Some parents recharge by reconnecting with friends or reviving pre-parenting hobbies. The key is finding what works for you.

The Power of Stepping Away

Stepping away isn't selfish; it's essential. Think of it like putting on your oxygen mask first. When you carve out time to recharge, you're better equipped to handle parenting's ups and downs, and you show your kids how to manage their own emotions. Here's why it matters:

- **Lower stress, sharper mind**: Regular breaks reduce stress and clear mental fog, helping you respond to challenges with patience. A 2010 study from University College London found that consistent stress-relief habits, like meditation or exercise, lower cortisol levels, boosting mental clarity.

- **Emotional balance**: Parenting is an emotional roller coaster—love, worry, frustration, all in one day. Stepping away helps you regulate those feelings, so you're steady for your kids.

- **Burnout protection**: Burnout can make even small tasks feel impossible. Research shows that self-care habits, like exercise or socializing, cut the risk of burnout and mental health struggles like anxiety.
- **More energy**: Your energy is finite. A quick walk or a quiet moment can recharge you, giving you the stamina to keep up with your kids.
- **Better health**: Exercise and relaxation improve mood, sleep, and fitness while lowering risks of chronic diseases. A Northern Ireland study linked parental exercise to better mental and physical health for both parents and kids.
- **Stronger relationships**: Time for yourself often means time for others—partners, friends, or new connections. These bonds provide emotional support, making parenting feel less isolating.
- **Bigger support network**: Social activities expand your circle, giving you more people to lean on for advice or a helping hand.

For kids, stepping away sets a powerful example:

- **Healthy habits**: When kids see you prioritize self-care or solve problems calmly, they learn to do the same.
- **Independence**: Giving yourself space lets kids practice independence, build confidence, and gain resilience.

The Relaxation Response

One of my favorite tools is the Relaxation Response, developed by cardiologist Herbert Benson in the 1970s. It's a simple meditation technique to calm the nervous system and counter stress's fight-or-flight effects. Benson found that focusing on a soothing word or phrase while breathing deeply for five to ten minutes, twice daily, can lower stress, blood pressure, and tension. With practice, it helps you stay calm even in chaotic moments. I teach clients to pick a word like "peace" or "calm," sit quietly, and let their breath anchor them. It's not for everyone, but it's a great starting point.

> **Meditation tip:** Start with five minutes in the morning. Focus on your breath and a calming word. If your mind wanders, gently bring it back. Try it for a month to feel the benefits.

The Road to Self-Care

Building self-care habits takes time, but it's worth it. Here's how to start:

1. **Start small:** Pick one small, doable habit that fits your life. If you're new to self-care, don't aim for an hour of yoga daily; start with five minutes. James Clear, in *Atomic Habits*, suggests "habit stacking," pairing a new habit with an existing one, like doing deep breathing after brushing your teeth. For example, if you want to read more, keep a book by your coffee maker and read a page while it brews. Small steps build momentum.

A client of mine started with ten minutes of stretching after dropping her kids at school. Within weeks, she felt more energized and added more time.

2. **Track progress:** Write down your goals and progress. Journaling keeps you accountable and helps you spot what works. Try scoring activities from 1 to 10 based on how they make you feel. One dad found that evening walks scored high for stress relief but low for energy, so he switched to morning jogs. Sharing your journal with a friend or therapist adds accountability. Apps like Habitica can also make tracking fun, turning habits into a game.

3. **Stay patient:** New habits take time, about sixty-six days to become automatic, according to a 2010 UCL study. If meditation feels awkward or running feels exhausting, give it a month before deciding it's not for you. Experiment with different activities—yoga, journaling, or even knitting—until you find your fit. Signing up for a class or doing an activity with a friend boosts commitment and adds social support. My client Sarah stuck with meditation despite early frustration, and after a month it became her go-to stress buster.

Real Parents, Real Results

Let's see how stepping away worked for some parents I've worked with. Their stories show that self-care isn't one-size-fits-all, but it's transformative when you find what clicks.

Sarah: Finding Calm in Meditation

Sarah, a mom of two and a marketing manager, was drowning in stress. Her days were a blur of meetings, school pickups, and bedtime battles. She was short-tempered and felt guilty for not being "present." I suggested meditation, starting with five minutes each morning. Sarah used Benson's Relaxation Response, focusing on the word "calm" while breathing deeply. She journaled her progress, noting how she felt before and after. Within weeks, she extended it to twenty minutes, finding it cleared her mind and steadied her emotions. During a heated argument with her son over homework, she paused, took a few deep breaths, and responded calmly, a win she credited to her practice. Her kids noticed her calmer vibe, and their home felt less tense.

> **Research note**: Studies show mindfulness reduces parental stress and improves family relationships. A 2019 study in *Frontiers in Psychology* found that mindfulness-based interventions lowered cortisol and boosted parent–child connection.

Mark: Running to Recharge

Mark, a single dad and software developer, struggled after going fully remote. Long hours at his desk left him drained, and his teenage son often came home to a grumpy dad. Mark missed outdoor time, so he started running twice daily: once in the morning, once after work. It was easy to fit into his routine since he no longer had school runs. On weekends, he and his son hiked nearby trails, bonding over shared adventures. Running boosted Mark's mood, energy, and sleep, making him more patient. His son opened up more on hikes, and their talks deepened their connection. Mark's stress dropped, and he felt healthier than he had in years.

> **Research note**: Exercise releases endorphins, reduces stress, and improves sleep. A study conducted in Northern Ireland linked parental exercise to better mental health for both parents and kids.

Lisa: Painting Her Way Back

Lisa, a stay-at-home mom of three, felt she'd lost herself in parenting. The constant demands—diapers, meals, and school projects—left her depressed and burned out. She tried yoga but found it meh. Then she remembered her college love for oil painting. Lisa carved out an hour every other evening to paint, setting up a corner in her garage. She joined a weekly art class, learning new techniques and making friends. Painting became her escape, reigniting her creativity and confidence. Her kids noticed her brighter mood and started asking about her artwork, sparking family art nights where they all painted together. Lisa's renewed energy made her more patient, and her home felt lighter.

> **Research note**: Numerous studies have confirmed enjoyable activities, creative or otherwise, reduce stress and boost overall well-being.

Jamie: Rebuilding Connections

Jamie, a high school teacher, moved to a new city with his partner and two kids. Without his old support network, he felt isolated, especially since his job surrounded him with teens, not adult friends. The loneliness amped up his stress, making him snappy at home. Jamie joined a local conservation group, spending weekends restoring trails. He also scheduled video calls with old friends from his hometown. These connections gave him a place to vent, laugh, and feel supported. His kids saw him happier, and his partner appreciated his lighter mood. Jamie's social outlets became his anchor, helping him tackle parenting with more resilience.

> **Research note**: Studies have found that parents with strong social connections and perceived social support report lower stress and greater life satisfaction.

Emily: Mindfulness for All

Emily, a mom of two teens, felt her family was struggling post-COVID. Her son and daughter bickered constantly, and communication with her husband was strained. Mindfulness had helped Emily manage her anxiety during the pandemic, so she introduced it to her family. They started with ten-minute morning sessions using a guided app. At first, her teens rolled their eyes, but the routine grew on them. The sessions became a calm start to the day, reducing arguments. Emily noticed her kids supporting each other more, like when her daughter helped her son with a school project. The family felt closer, and Emily's stress eased, knowing they were rebuilding their bond.

> **Research note**: Mindfulness fosters empathy and strengthens family ties. Zero to Three's resources show that mindfulness with young kids builds emotional regulation from an early age.

Anna: Therapy as a Lifeline

Anna, a corporate lawyer and mom of one, carried work stress home, snapping at her daughter and husband over small things. She tried exercise and meditation but felt too overwhelmed to stick with them. Reluctantly, she started therapy, worried it meant she was "failing." In sessions, Anna unpacked her stress, realizing many issues weren't as big as they seemed. Her therapist taught her visualization, picturing a calm beach to soothe her nerves during tense moments. Therapy gave Anna tools to pause and reframe challenges, like a work deadline or her daughter's tantrum. She became more patient, and her family noticed the change, with her daughter saying, "Mom, you're not mad all the time anymore."

> **Key takeaway**: It is well-known that therapy can help to reduce stress and optimize well-being. More specifically, cognitive behavioral therapy has been shown to help parents manage anxiety and strengthen family relationships.

Managing Stress in the Moment

Self-care builds a calm foundation, making high-stress moments, like a meltdown or a missed deadline, easier to handle. When stress hits, lean on your go-to habits. If meditation works, take a minute to breathe deeply, using Benson's Relaxation Response. If exercise is your thing, a quick walk can reset you. But what if your habit is painting or hiking? That's where visualization comes in.

Neuroscience shows that visualizing an activity, like swimming or painting, activates the same brain pathways as doing it. A client who loved woodworking couldn't bring his workshop to a stressful school meeting, but picturing himself sanding a table calmed him instantly. Try this: Close your eyes, imagine your favorite activity, and focus on the details, the sound of waves, the feel of a paintbrush. Even thirty seconds can lower your heart rate and clear your head.

> **Visualization tip**: Picture your happy place, say, a quiet forest or a cozy café. Focus on sights, sounds, and smells for one minute. Practice daily to make it a quick stress buster.

Building Resilience Through Self-Care

Self-care isn't just about feeling good; it's about building resilience for you and your kids. By prioritizing your well-being, you manage stress better, stay emotionally balanced, and model healthy habits. Whether it's Sarah's meditation, Mark's runs, or Lisa's painting, these habits recharge you, making parenting's chaos feel less overwhelming. Your kids learn from you, picking up skills like independence and emotional regulation that will carry them into adulthood.

As we move forward, we'll explore how to take these habits further, weaving them into a parenting approach that's both strong and flexible. What's one new habit that could create meaningful change for you and your family? The next chapter offers a fresh perspective that might just redefine how you face parenting's toughest days.

CHAPTER 4

What Is a Resilient Mindset?

Can you teach your mind to bend, not break, under parenting's pressures? Resilience isn't just about bouncing back; it's about growing stronger through the chaos. Many think resilience is something you're born with, like a natural knack for handling stress. But here's the truth: While everyone's stress tolerance varies, resilience is a skill you can build. As a clinical psychologist, I've helped countless parents strengthen their resilience, not just by changing habits but by shifting how they think.

Resilience has two pillars: lifestyle and mindset. So far, we've explored lifestyle habits like exercise, self-care, and social support that keep you steady. These are the foundation, helping you handle tantrums or tight deadlines with more calm. But a resilient mindset is the framework that holds it together. It's trusting you can tackle obstacles and picturing a positive outcome. Think of it as the mental muscle that turns "I can't do this" into "I'll figure it out."

This mindset draws from Carol Dweck's *Mindset: The New Psychology of Success*. Dweck's growth mindset, the belief that abilities can improve with effort, contrasts with a fixed mindset, where talents feel set in stone. A parent with a fixed mindset might think, "I'm just not patient" and give up. A parent with a growth mindset sees patience as something that can be learned and practices it daily. A resilient mindset builds on this, adding flexibility and optimism. It's not just about improving skills but seeing challenges as universal, manageable, and full of potential. Dweck's work shaped education and coaching, and it's a cornerstone of how I help parents.

Lifestyle and mindset are two sides of the same coin. Exercise or meditation strengthens your body and mind, making it easier to believe you can handle tough moments. Positive self-talk or journaling reinforces habits like daily walks. My approach is holistic, blending both to build resilience. I start with psychoeducation, showing parents how mindset shapes outcomes. Then we set SMART goals (Specific, Measurable, Achievable, Relevant, Time-bound), journal progress, and use cognitive behavioral techniques to reframe negative thoughts. Small steps, like a five-minute walk or a healthy snack, build confidence, proving change is possible.

In this chapter, we'll dive into the resilient mindset, exploring how it transforms parenting. Through real parents' stories, we'll see how mindset shifts, paired with practical tools, help you face hurdles with strength and hope.

> **Key takeaway**: A resilient mindset sees challenges as opportunities, not roadblocks, and pairs with lifestyle habits to build lasting strength.

Cami's Story: Rewiring for Resilience

Cami, a marketing executive and mom of three, was stretched to her limit. Work deadlines, kids' schedules, and endless chores left her frazzled and down. She'd tried talk therapy, which felt too abstract, and cognitive behavioral therapy, which helped her understand thoughts but didn't ease daily stress. She needed tools that worked in her chaotic life.

Finding Practical Tools

We started with mindfulness, practicing five-minute breathing sessions each morning. Cami journaled her stress triggers—late meetings, sibling fights—and how she felt after meditating. She set boundaries, like no work emails after 7 p.m., to protect family time. Self-care became nonnegotiable: a weekly yoga class and a daily ten-minute walk. These steps weren't just habits; they built her belief that she could handle her load.

Shifting Perspective

To foster a resilient mindset, we used positive self-talk. Cami practiced daily affirmations, like "I'm doing my best, and that's enough." When she snapped at her kids, she reframed it: "I messed up, but I can try again." Journaling her "daily wins" boosted her confidence. Over the months, Cami became more patient, focused at work, and fulfilled. Her kids noticed, saying, "Mom, you're happier now." By blending lifestyle changes with mindset shifts, Cami transformed her parenting.

> **Key takeaway**: Small, intentional habits and positive self-talk can rewire your mindset, making daily challenges feel manageable.

Building Your Resilient Mindset

Now that we've seen Cami's transformation, let's unpack how you can build that same mindset. These practices, grounded in research, help you see obstacles as stepping stones.

Believe in Your Resilience

Start by trusting that resilience can be learned. You're not stuck with your current stress response; you can grow stronger. Reflect on past wins: Maybe you handled a toddler's meltdown, juggled a work crisis, or managed a challenge at home. Those moments prove you're capable. Write down one tough moment you overcame to remind yourself of your strength and ability to handle hard things. And remember, believing in the possibility on the other side of challenge is always important.

Embrace a Growth Mindset

See challenges as chances to learn. When things go wrong, like a missed school event, ask, "What can I gain from this?" Maybe it's better planning or self-compassion. Journaling helps: Note one challenge weekly and what you learned. Dweck's research shows that this reframing builds motivation and persistence. For example, instead of "I'm a bad parent for yelling," try "Yelling shows I'm stressed, so I'll practice pausing next time."

> **Daily wins exercise**: Each night, write three to five things that went well, like staying calm or making your kid laugh. This shifts focus to progress, boosting your optimism.

Use Positive Self-Talk

Your inner voice shapes your reality. Swap "I'm failing" for "I'm learning." Try five-minute mirror talks: Say things like "I'm strong enough for this" or "I am doing my best." A client, frustrated with her picky eater, started saying, "I'm helping my son try new foods." It eased her stress and made mealtimes calmer. A 2019 study in *The Journal of Positive Psychology* linked positive self-talk and overall self-efficacy to lower levels of stress and higher confidence.

Tune Into Emotions

Parenting stirs big feelings: joy, worry, and guilt. Ignoring them can sap your resilience. Notice how you feel during tough moments. If you're overwhelmed, pause and name it: "I'm stressed because bedtime's a mess." This awareness, backed by mindfulness studies, helps you respond, not react. A ten-second breath can reset you.

Practice Patience

Patience is a resilience superpower. Stepping away, like going for a quick walk, gives perspective. If you rush through story time, slow down intentionally. Ask: *Am I patient in calm moments?* Practicing patience daily, like waiting calmly when your kid ties their shoes, prepares you for high-pressure situations.

> **Key takeaway**: Building a resilient mindset starts with believing you can grow, reframing challenges and practicing patience daily.

Rachel and Temu's Story: Facing a Child's Illness

Rachel and Temu's world shifted when their ten-year-old son, Peter, was diagnosed with type 1 diabetes. Suddenly, parenting meant monitoring blood sugar, giving insulin shots, and worrying about emergencies. The emotional weight, fear for Peter's future, and guilt over his struggles were heavy.

Managing Worry

Rachel and Temu's biggest hurdle was fear. Would Peter live a normal life? Could they manage his care? They joined an online support group for parents of kids with diabetes, meeting families who thrived despite the condition. Hearing their stories shifted Rachel's mindset: "If they can do this, so can we." The group offered practical tips, like meal planning, and emotional support, easing their isolation. A 2021 study in *Diabetes Care* found that support groups boost parental confidence and reduce stress.

Building Routine

Before Peter's diagnosis, their home was disorganized, meals were haphazard, schedules loose. Diabetes demanded structure. They set fixed times for meals, blood sugar checks, and insulin. Each morning, they involved Peter, teaching him to read his glucose meter. This routine wasn't just practical; it gave Peter agency and his parents peace of mind. A 2022 study in *Frontiers in Pediatrics* found that structure and preparation help parents feel more in control and less overwhelmed in caring for a child with a chronic illness.

Encouraging Autonomy

Rachel worried about hovering but knew Peter needed independence. They let him play soccer and swim, adjusting insulin as needed. They praised his efforts, like learning to check his sugar alone, building his confidence. Peter's resilience grew; he even explained diabetes to friends, proud of his knowledge. Encouraging autonomy, research shows, fosters self-efficacy in kids.

Prioritizing Self-Care

To stay strong, Rachel and Temu kept up their bike rides and yoga, taking one night weekly for friends. Modeling self-care showed Ethan it's important to prioritize well-being. Their resilience inspired Peter, who adapted to his routine and managed his condition with growing confidence. Rachel said, "Seeing him thrive makes every hard day worth it."

> **Key takeaway**: A resilient mindset, paired with routine and support, helps parents and kids face serious challenges with hope.

Eni and Mike's Story: Navigating Divorce

Divorce is tough on kids, stirring sadness, anger, or guilt. Eni and Mike, after fifteen years of marriage, faced this with their kids, Onel (twelve) and Emme (eight). Onel withdrew, struggling at school, while Emme had anxiety-driven outbursts. Eni and Mike wanted to ease the transition, staying resilient for their kids.

Creating Stability

We reviewed research showing kids can adapt to divorce with thoughtful parenting. Eni and Mike built a stable routine, consistent bedtimes, shared meals, and clear custody schedules. They used the same rules at both homes, giving Onel and Emme predictability.

Communicating Positively

They agreed to speak positively about each other and the divorce, saying, "We both love you, and that won't change." Therapy helped them process emotions privately, avoiding slipups. They used consistent language, reassuring the kids they weren't to blame. This, according to research by the Family Institute at Northwestern University, fosters security in kids.

Celebrating Together

Eni and Mike attended birthdays and school events as a team, showing Onel and Emme they were still a family. Self-care, like Eni's weekly runs and Mike's therapy, kept them grounded. Over time, Onel opened up, and Emme's outbursts eased. The kids saw their parents' resilience, learning to adapt with confidence.

> **Key takeaway**: Resilient co-parenting, with routine and positive communication, helps kids thrive through divorce.

Mike's Solo Journey: Overcoming Self-Doubt

Mike, from the divorce story, faced his mindset challenge. Post-separation, he doubted his parenting, feeling he wasn't "enough" for Onel and Emme. We worked on reframing: Instead of "I'm failing them," he tried "I'm learning to parent solo." He journaled daily wins, like making Emme laugh or helping Onel with homework. Setting SMART goals, like one tech-free evening weekly, built his confidence. Mike's shift to a resilient mindset made him more present, and his kids felt his renewed strength.

> **Key takeaway**: Reframing self-doubt with small wins and clear goals builds a parent's resilience.

Your Path to Resilience

Building a resilient mindset takes practice, but it's transformative. Start small: Try the daily wins exercise or a five-minute mirror talk. Experiment with what feels right: journaling, affirmations, or a quick walk. Pair these with lifestyle habits like exercise or meditation for a holistic approach. Your mindset shapes not just you, but also your kids, who learn resilience by watching you. There's no shortcut, but every step forward strengthens your family.

How is it possible to turn your toughest moments into your greatest strengths? The next chapter explores the mindset shifts and actions that can open new possibilities in your parenting.

CHAPTER 5

Challenges Are Everywhere

How do you know when to jump in and fix your child's problems or let them figure it out? Every kid faces hurdles, from small stumbles like tying shoelaces to big struggles like academic pressure or bullying. As parents, you want to guide them, ease their disappointment, and help them grow through both wins and setbacks. But striking that balance, knowing when to step in or step back, is tricky, especially as kids grow more independent. In this chapter, we'll explore how to equip your kids with skills to tackle obstacles, create a home where it's safe to fail, and support them through common challenges like school struggles, social drama, and self-esteem dips.

When to Step In

Parenting is a dance of involvement and independence. You want to support your kids without hovering, guide them without solving everything. Stepping in too soon can rob them of problem-solving skills, but waiting too long might leave them overwhelmed. The key is teaching them to handle challenges while showing they can lean on you. For example, when my son struggled with advanced math freshman year, failing tests despite hard work, his confidence suffered. We couldn't switch his class midyear, and neither my husband nor I could teach advanced math. Instead of taking over, we helped him set up teacher meetings and tutoring. Those steps empowered him to succeed, teaching him that challenges are normal and surmountable with support.

What Counts as a Challenge

Challenges come in all sizes. For a toddler, it's mastering a zipper. For a teen, it's navigating peer drama or exams. No matter the scale, every hurdle feels big to a kid facing it for the first time. Don't brush off "small" problems like missing a team tryout or being left out of a party; these can hit hard, shaping how kids handle rejection or perseverance. Validating their feelings builds resilience and shows them it's okay to struggle. As a clinical psychologist, I see parents seeking help for issues like academic stress, learning differences, bullying, anxiety, or low self-esteem. The strategies we use for everyday setbacks—problem-solving, self-awareness, asking for help—also apply to these bigger struggles.

Why Failure Builds Resilience

Failure isn't the enemy; it's a teacher. Kids who learn to navigate setbacks develop independence and a stronger sense of self. When they confront issues, like bombing a test or losing a friend, they discover what they're capable of and when to seek help. Your role is to guide, not rescue. Create a home where mistakes are safe, effort is celebrated, and asking for help is a strength. This mindset helps kids see challenges as chances to grow, not proof they're not enough.

Common Challenges and How to Help

Let's dive into the challenges I see most in my practice and how you can support your kids through them.

Academic Challenges

School struggles are a top reason parents seek help. Kids develop at different paces, with unique strengths and needs. Some breeze through math; others hit walls. If your child is falling behind, pinpoint the cause: Maybe it's a tough subject, stress, or a learning difference like dyslexia. Work with teachers and, if needed, specialists to create a plan. Pressure from parents, teachers, or society can backfire, making kids anxious rather than motivated. Remind them that learning matters more than grades and home is a safe space to celebrate effort.

Learning differences, like dyslexia or dyscalculia, affect many kids. Schools now offer better support, like individualized education plans (IEPs). Don't hesitate to advocate for accommodations; extra test time, audiobooks, or tutoring can make a huge difference. A 2020 study in *Journal of Learning Disabilities* found that tailored interventions boost academic outcomes and confidence for kids with learning differences.

Overcoming Learning Difficulties: Ashley's Story
Ashley, a ten-year-old who loved drawing and fantasy books, dreaded school. Reading and math were tough, sapping her confidence. She'd hide her homework, fearing failure, and cry before class. Her teacher suspected a learning difference, and tests confirmed dyslexia, which made reading and language processing hard.

Building Confidence
Ashley's parents teamed up with her school for an Individualized Education Program (IEP), securing extra test time, one-on-one reading sessions, and audiobooks. They hired a dyslexia-specialized tutor who taught Ashley techniques like chunking words. At home, her parents praised her effort—drawing, reading short stories—and avoided focusing on grades.

Celebrating Progress
Ashley's skills grew, and so did her courage. She read aloud in class, a feat she once avoided, and joined a book club, feeling proud. Her parents' support—validating her struggles, securing help—helped her see her potential. By year's end, Ashley tackled assignments with less fear, knowing her unique learning style was her strength. Parents can support academic struggles by securing tailored accommodations and celebrating small wins.

Social Challenges

Navigating friendships is a minefield, especially as kids hit adolescence and social lives become more private. Learning your child feels left out, bullied, or socially anxious is gut-wrenching. It's tough to help when they won't open up or when you have little sway over their world. Balance trusting them to handle issues with stepping in if their well-being suffers.

Social skills vary. Shy or introverted kids may struggle to connect, while others dive in easily. Parents can help by exposing them to different settings—sports, art classes, or clubs—where they can find their fit. Model healthy social habits, like active listening, to show them how to build bonds.

Bullying—physical, verbal, or online—can impact a child's mental health. Kids often hide it, so watch for mood swings, school avoidance, or anxiety. If you suspect bullying, talk calmly, involve teachers as needed, and consider consulting a therapist.

> ### Overcoming Bullying: Lila's Story
> Lila, a twelve-year-old soccer fan, was outgoing until seventh grade, when a group of girls started targeting her. They made fun of her clothes in group chats and excluded her at lunch. Lila grew quiet, skipped practices, and faked being sick to avoid school. Her parents noticed her spark fading but didn't know why.
>
> ### Opening Communication
> Lila's mom asked open-ended questions—"How's school feeling?"—and learned about the bullying. They met with her teacher, who monitored the girls'

behavior and addressed bullying. Lila's parents enrolled her in a weekend art class, a safe space to make new friends.

Rebuilding Confidence
The art class helped Lila connect with kids who shared her interests. Her parents praised her resilience, like attending class despite having anxiety, and taught her to set boundaries, like ignoring cruel texts. By the end of the semester, Lila rejoined soccer, feeling stronger. Her parents' calm support and proactive steps helped her reclaim her confidence.

Mental Health Challenges

Anxiety and depression are rising among kids, often tied to school pressure or social struggles. Anxiety shows as excessive worry, irritability, or physical symptoms like headaches and stomach aches. Depression may look like sadness, withdrawal, or irritability. Kids can mask these symptoms, so stay alert for changes in behavior or interests.

If you suspect anxiety or depression, consult a specialist. Cognitive behavioral therapy (CBT) or social skills training can help in most cases. CBT teaches kids to understand and manage the connection between their thoughts, feelings and behaviors. Treatment of separation anxiety, common in younger kids, often combines CBT with gradual exposure to build independence and confidence.

Common Mental Health Signs

- **Anxiety**: Excessive worry, fearfulness, irritability, clinginess, headaches, fatigue, sleep issues, rapid heartbeat. Therapy with an emphasis on CBT and coping skills can help.

- **Social anxiety**: Avoiding social situations, isolation. CBT or social skills groups help.

- **Generalized anxiety**: Worry across many areas, disrupting daily life. Professional support and parenting strategies ease it.

- **Separation anxiety**: Fear of leaving parents or home, common in young kids. Gradual exposure builds confidence.

- **Depression**: Sadness, irritability, loss of interest. Therapy, medication, and family support are key.
  Consult a specialist to address root causes and tailor treatment.

Self-Esteem

Low self-esteem fuels anxiety, depression, and social struggles. Kids with shaky self-worth may doubt their abilities or avoid risks. Build their confidence by celebrating strengths, kindness, humor, and effort, not just results. Let them fail safely, learning they can bounce back. If issues with self-esteem persist, explore the cause with a therapist.

> **Support Through Social Anxiety: Tommy's Story**
> Tommy, an eight-year-old with a curious mind, hid

his social struggles behind a cheerful smile. In preschool, he played alone, overwhelmed by groups. By second grade, he grew irritable about school, avoiding class discussions. His parents worried he would fall behind socially.

Learning Social Skills
We used role-playing games to teach Tommy eye contact, conversation starters, and reading emotions. He practiced in therapy but struggled at school. His parents enrolled him in a social skills group, where he met kids facing similar hurdles, easing his loneliness.

A Furry Friend's Impact
Max, a therapy dog, visited Tommy's class weekly. Tommy bonded with Max instantly, his anxiety fading in the dog's presence. He started joining group activities, even making friends. For the school play, Tommy performed with Max by his side, a huge step. His confidence grew, and he felt less alone. Parents can ease social anxiety by connecting kids with supportive peers and creative outlets like therapy dogs.

Research note: A 2018 study in the *Journal of Pediatric Nursing* showed how therapy dogs reduce anxiety and boost social growth in kids, their calming presence helps kids like Tommy engage.

The Resilient Parent: Your Role

Supporting your kids starts with you. Resilient parents are emotionally available, communicate openly, and empathize with their kids' needs. This ties to the resilient parenting skills we've explored: self-care, stepping away, support networks, and role modeling.

- **Self-care**: Prioritize your well-being to stay energized. A daily walk or quiet moment keeps you steady for your kids.
- **Stepping away**: Pause to assess your child's struggles objectively. Overreacting or ignoring issues can miss the mark. A clear head helps you choose the right support.
- **Support networks**: Lean on teachers, therapists, or family when things get tough. For example, if your teen won't talk to you, a trusted coach or relative can bridge the gap. It is well known that strong networks can reduce parental stress.
- **Role modeling**: Show resilience by handling your setbacks calmly. Kids learn by watching you recover from a bad day or solve a problem.

Every child's journey is unique, but by validating their struggles, securing help, and modeling resilience, you build a tool kit they'll carry for life. You grow too, strengthening your bond through shared challenges.

What's one parenting strategy that could change how your child faces their toughest moments? The next chapter explores how to strengthen their resilience, and yours.

CHAPTER 6

Emotionally Intelligent Parenting

Ever wonder why some parenting moments feel like a breeze while others leave you frazzled? The difference often comes down to emotionally intelligent parenting: knowing your emotions, managing them wisely, and tuning into your kids' feelings with empathy. Nobody's perfect at this. You might feel a deep connection with one child but struggle with another or find it easy to express joy but hard to handle anger. That's okay. Emotional intelligence isn't about perfection; it's about growing through practice. In this chapter, we'll explore what emotionally intelligent parenting looks like, why it builds resilience, and how you can use practical tools to nurture it in yourself and your kids.

What Is Emotionally Intelligent Parenting?

Emotionally intelligent parenting means understanding and managing your emotions while recognizing and responding to your child's feelings thoughtfully. It's about staying calm during a tantrum, empathizing with a teen's heartbreak, and fostering a home where everyone feels heard. Drawing from Daniel Goleman's work, emotional intelligence has five key components:

1. **Self-awareness**: Knowing your emotions, strengths, and triggers, and how they shape your actions.
2. **Empathy**: Feeling what others feel, showing compassion, and responding with care.
3. **Self-regulation**: Staying composed under stress, controlling impulses, and focusing on solutions.
4. **Motivation**: Channeling emotions to pursue goals with drive and optimism.
5. **Social skills**: Communicating clearly, resolving conflicts, and building strong relationships through listening and cooperation.

These skills help you navigate the ups and downs of parenting while teaching your kids to do the same. I have observed in my practice over the past twenty years that emotional intelligence is a powerful variable for managing challenges. A 2023 study in *Frontiers of Public Health* found that parents with a higher level of emotional intelligence experience increased feelings of parental competence and connection with their kids.

Why It Builds Resilience

Now that we've defined emotional intelligence, let's see why it builds resilience. When you understand your emotions, you stay steady during chaos, like a toddler's meltdown or a teen's defiance.

This calm helps you find healthy ways to vent frustration, like a walk or deep breaths, instead of snapping. By tuning into your kids' feelings, you de-escalate conflicts, offer support, and guide them through crises. This builds their resilience, too; they learn to name emotions, solve problems, and bounce back. Overall research in this area has shown that kids with emotionally intelligent parents are more adaptable and less anxious.

Emotionally intelligent parenting also models resilience. When you handle a mishap with grace, say, laughing off a spilled coffee instead of getting upset, your kids see how to recover from setbacks. This creates a home where mistakes are safe, and growth is celebrated.

Emotional Competence in Action

Emotional intelligence is the understanding; emotional competence is the doing. It's acting on your awareness, expressing emotions constructively, responding to your kids' feelings with empathy, and handling tense moments effectively. Many parents have the awareness but hesitate to act. Take my client who saw her teen son struggling after a move. She knew he was upset about leaving friends but didn't know how to reach him. Her frustration grew, widening their disconnect. This is common; parents sense their kids' emotions but fear making things worse or aren't used to open emotional talks.

Emotional competence requires practice, like any skill. It's responding to a child's anger with, "I see you're upset; let's talk," instead of yelling back. It's validating a teen's sadness without rushing to fix it. By acting on your emotional intelligence, you build trust and strengthen your bond.

Practical Tools for Emotionally Intelligent Parenting

So, how do you grow your emotional intelligence and put it into action? Here are five key practices to start today:

1. **Reflect regularly**: Journal, talk with a friend, or pause to process your emotions. Write down what happened in your day, where you were, who you saw, and how it felt. This builds awareness and helps you spot emotional patterns. Try prompts like, "What frustrated me today, and why?" or "When did I feel closest to my kid?"

2. **Practice mindfulness**: Sit quietly for five minutes, focus on your breath, and let thoughts pass without judgment. Apps like Headspace or Calm guide beginners. Mindfulness practice boosts self-regulation, helping you stay calm during stress.

3. **Observe mindfully**: Watch your kids during play or homework. Notice their expressions, tone, and actions to understand their emotions. This sharpens empathy and helps you respond thoughtfully, like asking, "You seem quiet; everything okay?"

4. **Listen actively**: Give your kids your full attention, with eye contact and no interruptions. Reflect what they say: "Sounds like you're upset about that test." Journal

afterward: "What did I learn about my child?" This builds trust and empathy.

5. **Respond empathetically**: Use phrases like, "I get how tough this is," or share a similar experience to connect. Offer solutions only after validating feelings. This fosters open communication and emotional growth.

These tools work across parenting stages. With young kids, you'll practice in tantrums or playtime. With teens, you'll navigate mood swings and independence. Keep learning; read books like *Emotional Intelligence Habits* by Travis Bradberry or *Master Your Emotions* by Thibaut Meurisse.

Real-Life Applications

Let's see emotionally intelligent parenting in action through parents who used these tools to transform their relationships.

Maria's Story: Breaking Through with Active Listening

Maria's twelve-year-old son, Alex, grew distant, skipping soccer and sulking at home. She'd always encouraged open talks, but Alex clammed up. Worried, Maria carved out one-on-one time, driving him to baseball practice weekly.

Building Trust

Maria practiced active listening, asking, "How's school going?" and waiting patiently. After weeks of small talk, she gently asked, "What's been tough lately?" Alex admitted a group of boys was bullying him, leaving him ashamed. Maria listened without interrupting, saying, "That sounds really hard; you're brave to share." She shared her own school struggles, building trust.

Taking Action
With Alex's okay, Maria contacted his school to address the bullying. They brainstormed ways to handle it. In time, Alex's confidence returned, and he rejoined soccer. Maria's empathetic listening opened the door to solutions, strengthening their bond. Parents can connect with a withdrawn child by listening patiently and validating feelings.

Rich's Story: Regulating Emotions for Better Parenting
Rich, a dad of three, prided himself on firm parenting. His "no whining" rule worked with Liam (ten) and Nora (seven), but four-year-old Zoe's tantrums tested him. His stern responses, time-outs, and raised voice escalated her outbursts, leaving Rich feeling upset and guilty.

Learning Emotional Control
Rich started mindful observation, journaling Zoe's tantrums. He noticed they spiked when her siblings competed for attention. Next time Zoe melted down, Rich took deep breaths, knelt to her level, and asked, "Are you mad because Nora interrupted?" He validated her feelings: "It's okay to feel upset."

Teaching Calm
Rich taught Zoe to blow bubbles through a wand, a fun way to breathe deeply. They'd talk after,

pinpointing what sparked her anger. Zoe's tantrums lessened, and Rich felt calmer. His emotional regulation modeled resilience for Zoe. Parents can de-escalate tantrums by staying calm and teaching kids simple calming tools.

Mark and Elena's Story: Motivating with Positive Reinforcement

Mark and Elena's ten-year-old, Noah, was a bundle of energy but struggled to focus in school. Teachers flagged his disruptive behavior, and the couple's initial scolding hurt Noah's confidence. They worried it'd dent his self-esteem.

Shifting to Positivity

Mark and Elena created a star chart, rewarding Noah for tasks like finishing homework or listening in class. Five stars earned a small treat, like a toy or ice cream. They praised his effort, saying, "You worked hard on that math!" Noah's motivation soared, and he felt proud.

Seeing Results

Noah's behavior improved, and he tackled school with more focus. Mark and Elena's positive reinforcement built his resilience, showing him that setbacks are temporary. Parents can boost a child's confidence by rewarding effort and celebrating small wins.

Camila's Story: Respecting Teen Boundaries

Camila set a strict curfew for her teen son, Alvaro, to keep him safe. At fifteen, Alvaro pushed back, staying out late and sneaking out, sparking arguments. Camila's worry turned to frustration, straining their bond.

Finding Balance
Camila practiced active listening, asking Alvaro why he wanted more freedom. She shared her concerns calmly, saying, "I worry when I don't know where you are." They agreed on a weekday curfew but looser weekend rules if Alvaro shared his plans.

Building Trust
Alvaro respected the deal, and Camila worried less, trusting his choices. Their open communication rebuilt trust, giving Alvaro independence and Camila peace. Parents can navigate teen rebellion by listening, setting clear rules, and compromising.

Lila's Story: Teaching Empathy Through Experience
Lila, a mom of eight-year-old Sophie, noticed Sophie was unkind to a shy classmate, Mia, often excluding her at recess. Lila wanted Sophie to become more empathic but didn't want to lecture.

Fostering Empathy
Lila used mindful observation during Sophie's playdates, noting her interactions. She asked, "How do you think Mia feels when she's left out?" and shared a story of feeling excluded as a kid. Lila also enrolled Sophie in a community service club, where she helped younger kids, learning to care for others.

Seeing Growth
Sophie started inviting Mia to play, noticing her smiles. Lila praised her kindness, as Sophie's actions

showed she understood others' feelings. Parents can teach empathy by guiding kids to reflect on others' emotions and act compassionately.

The Lifelong Payoff of Emotionally Intelligent Parenting

Emotionally intelligent parenting transforms your family. Reflecting regularly builds self-awareness, helping you stay calm. Practicing empathy and active listening creates trust, making kids feel safe to share. Positive reinforcement and emotional regulation foster resilience, teaching kids to handle setbacks. These skills don't just help now; they strengthen bonds for life. Numerous studies suggest that children raised by parents with high emotional intelligence are more likely to develop stronger emotional regulation skills, healthier self-esteem, and secure attachment. Decades of research in developmental psychology have linked these traits to better peer relationships, romantic stability, and well-adjusted adult functioning.

You'll never be perfect, and that's fine. Parenting is messy, with calm days and tense ones. The parents in these stories—Maria, Rich, Mark, Elena, Camila, and Lila—showed that intentional practice makes a difference. You're building a blueprint for your kids' emotional lives, helping them thrive in their relationships long after they leave home.

What emotional skills can help your family move through its toughest moments with greater strength and connection? The next chapter explores how to build resilience together, one moment at a time.

CHAPTER 7

Building Resilience Is a Process

Resilience is a journey, not a race. It's about taking small, intentional steps rather than chasing drastic overhauls. Many parents hope for a quick fix to life's challenges, but real change unfolds gradually, weaving through the complexities of daily life. The good news? Small changes can spark big results, giving you more energy, clarity, and connection with your kids.

Some parents find comfort in knowing resilience is a process. It eases the pressure when progress isn't instant, and focusing on bite-sized goals feels doable. Others, though, hear "process" and feel overwhelmed; parenting is already a full plate, and adding more tasks can seem daunting. If that's you, here's the key: Resilience isn't about piling on more. It's about finding smarter ways to approach parenting, with more empathy, patience, and perspective. These changes pay off, freeing up mental space and boosting your ability to handle whatever comes your way.

In this chapter, I'll guide you through practical steps to weave resilience into your life, where to start, how to build momentum, and how to celebrate progress. Let's dive in with a road map that's flexible enough to fit your unique routine.

Finding Your Path to Resilience

So, how do you build resilience? It starts with small, meaningful steps, clear goals, and moments of reflection to track your progress. Here are four principles to guide you:

- Fit changes into your existing routine for seamless integration.
- Choose habits that resonate with you; belief in their value keeps you committed.
- Stay accountable, whether through a journal, a friend, or a coach.
- Adapt the process to suit your life; there's no one-size-fits-all.

Think of resilience like building a house. A strong foundation (your physical and emotional health) supports everything else: self-esteem, awareness, and connection with others. With these in place, you're better equipped to parent with mindfulness and positivity. Creating a road map helps. Some parents love mapping out long-term goals up front; others prefer setting smaller targets as they go. Either way, keep the big picture in mind: Resilience strengthens you *and* your family, shifting how you navigate challenges together.

Part One: The Resilience Road Map

Here's a sample road map inspired by parents I've worked with. It's not a rigid plan; think of it as a starting point to adapt to your life.

1. Boost Health and Fitness

Health is often the first thing parents neglect, yet it's the bedrock of resilience. Better health means more energy, a brighter mood, and sharper emotional regulation. Here's how to start small:

- **Hydrate daily.** Most of us skimp on water. Drinking a full glass at a set time—say, with breakfast—boosts energy and focus.
- **Swap one food.** Balanced meals matter, but they're tough to stick to. Try replacing one unhealthy snack (like chips) with a nutrient-packed option (like an apple). It's a double win: more good stuff, less junk.
- **Move for ten to thirty minutes.** Pick an activity you enjoy: walking, dancing, or even chasing your kids around the park. Movement lifts your mood and builds stamina.
- **Set a bedtime routine.** A consistent wind-down ritual signals your body to rest. Try reading or stretching for ten minutes before bed; it becomes second nature.

These steps lay the foundation for resilience, giving you the energy to tackle parenting with confidence. When you feel better physically, your kids benefit from your brighter, more present self.

2. Manage Stress with Mindfulness

Health isn't just physical; it's mental too. Stress can erode your patience, so carving out moments to recharge is key. Instead of scrolling during breaks, try:

- **Deep breathing.** Take five slow breaths during lunch or coffee breaks to calm your nervous system.
- **Short walks.** A ten-minute stroll can reset your mind.
- **Mindfulness moments.** Focus on the present; savor your tea or notice the breeze. These small pauses build calm over time.

Regular mindfulness lowers your baseline stress, equipping you to handle tough moments with clarity. This benefits your kids too; less stress in you means a calmer, more connected home.

3. Raise Self-Awareness and Set Goals

Self-awareness is your compass. Journaling for five to twenty minutes daily or weekly helps you spot what triggers stress or sparks joy. Write down:

- What sets you off (e.g., a messy house, work deadlines).
- What lifts you up (e.g., a chat with a friend, a quiet moment).
- Goals for the week, like trying one new habit or reflecting on progress.

This practice sharpens your focus on what works, letting you adjust as you go. It also models self-reflection for your kids, teaching them to navigate their own emotions.

4. Strengthen Your Social Network

Connection fuels resilience. Whether it's coffee with a friend, family dinners, or joining a community group, relationships recharge you. Reflect on what fulfills you; maybe it's reconnecting with old friends or meeting new ones. One parent I know joined a toddler gym class expecting just a fun activity for her twins. Seventeen years later, she's still close with the parents she met there, sharing advice and support.

4.1 Use Your Social Support

Don't just build connections; lean on them. Map out your network: Who can watch your kids for an hour or share carpool duties? Asking for help isn't a weakness; it's a strategy. Many parents are surprised by how much support is out there once they ask. This lightens your load, giving you space to parent with more patience and presence.

5. Create Boundaries with Technology

Phones are double-edged swords, helpful but addictive. To keep them in check:

- **Turn off notifications.** Silence nonessential alerts to reduce distractions.
- **Keep phones out of the bedroom.** Charge them elsewhere to protect your sleep.
- **Go phone-free weekly.** Try a walk or outing without your device. It's liberating.

These boundaries free up mental space, letting you engage more fully with your kids and yourself. A clearer mind means a more intentional approach to parenting.

6. Find Time for Hobbies

Hobbies aren't frivolous; they're fuel. Whether it's gardening, running, or painting, activities you love boost confidence and joy. Ask yourself: What makes me feel alive? Even thirty minutes a week can recharge you. Many hobbies double as exercise or social time, amplifying their benefits. Prioritizing "you time" sets a powerful example for your kids about balance and fulfillment.

Quick Checklist for Resilience:

- Drink water daily.
- Swap one unhealthy snack.
- Move ten to thirty minutes daily.
- Set a bedtime routine.
- Practice mindfulness breaks.
- Journal to track triggers and goals.
- Nurture social connections.
- Set tech boundaries.
- Make time for hobbies.

These steps build a foundation that strengthens you and your family, paving the way for a new approach to parenting.

Part Two: Approach Parenting from a New Angle

Resilience transforms how you parent. By focusing on your health, mindfulness, and connections, you gain a fresh perspective, more positive, patient, and present. Here's how parents I've worked with have shifted their approach.

1. Give the Gift of Independence

Stepping back to focus on yourself gives your kids room to grow. Age-appropriate independence builds their confidence and yours.

> **Eve's story**: Eve, a single mom, hovered over her fourteen-year-old daughter, Sofia, to keep her safe. But Sofia's rebellion, skipping classes or sneaking out, left Eve stressed. To prioritize her health, Eve started going to the gym, leaving Sofia home alone for short periods. That small step was a game changer. Sofia took on more responsibilities, like tidying the kitchen, and her confidence soared. Eve found that trusting Sofia strengthened their bond, easing her own anxiety and creating a more harmonious home. This shift benefited both; Sofia grew more independent, and Eve parented with greater calm.

2. Compartmentalize Your Life

Stress from work or life can spill into parenting. Mindfulness helps you draw boundaries, keeping those stressors in check.

Kaja's story: Kaja, a project manager and mom of two boys, often snapped at her sons over small issues like messy rooms. She realized work stress, especially tense coworker dynamics, was bleeding into home life. Through therapy, Kaja used mindfulness to separate the two. A ten-minute meditation before leaving work helped her "reset" for home. She also journaled to pinpoint stress triggers, which let her approach her boys with patience. This shift created a calmer home, where her sons felt heard rather than scolded.

3. Take a Positive Approach

Your mood sets the tone for your family. Investing in your well-being, through exercise, hobbies, or friendships, sparks positivity that ripples outward.

Anna's story: After a career setback, Anna's confidence took a hit. She became overly critical of her two sons' choices, from clothes to friends, creating tension at home. Seeking fulfillment, Anna joined a local field hockey club as a coach, a sport she loved. Coaching rebuilt her self-esteem, and she began seeing her sons' choices as expressions of their individuality, not as flaws. Her positivity transformed their home, her boys opened up more, and Anna felt less guilt, knowing her happiness lifted the whole family.

4. Try a Different Approach

Resilience opens your mind to new parenting strategies, benefiting everyone.

> **James's story**: James, a dad of three, grew up with strict discipline and used the same with his kids, believing it taught respect. But his children grew withdrawn, hesitant to share. Frustrated, James explored positive discipline, focusing on encouragement and mutual respect. He set clear expectations, praised good behavior, and involved his kids in problem-solving, like creating a chore chart together. The results were striking: His kids became more cooperative, less fearful, and eager to talk. James felt closer to them, realizing that respect built through connection was stronger than fear-based discipline. This shift not only improved behavior but deepened their trust, making family life richer and more open.

5. Embrace Your Unique Context

Resilience helps you accept your family's unique journey, without unhealthy comparisons.

> **Lina's story**: Lina struggled with her daughter Mia's ADHD, which made outings like dinners or errands exhausting. Comparing herself to other parents left her frustrated. Through therapy and a support group, Lina learned to embrace Mia's needs. She created a structured routine—dedicated times for homework, play, and rest—and focused on Mia's strengths, like her love for drawing and soccer. These

activities became family bonding moments. Lina's shift in perspective, celebrating Mia's uniqueness, built Mia's confidence and made outings less stressful. Lina found joy in their distinct path, knowing she was supporting Mia's growth.

The Wheel of Change Gains Momentum

Change isn't instant, and it takes effort across multiple fronts. But here's the beauty: When you prioritize your health, mindfulness, and connections, you create a ripple effect. A stronger you means a stronger family. Think of change like pushing a heavy wheel over bumpy ground. At first, it's tough, but once it starts rolling, momentum builds. Some days, the wheel glides; others, it needs a nudge. Resilience keeps it moving, helping you face challenges with clarity and compassion.

Why is it so important to focus on your strengths within your own unique context? The next chapter explores the power of appreciating who you are without comparison or unrealistic expectations.

CHAPTER 8

Celebrating Your Own Unique Context

Your family is one of a kind. Even if you think you blend into the crowd, take a closer look; your challenges, joys, and quirks tell a story no one else shares. Parenting advice bombards us with images of "perfect" families, but chasing that ideal is a trap. Instead, celebrating what makes your family special lifts the pressure to conform. This chapter shows how self-awareness and compassion help you embrace your unique context, parent authentically, and build resilience for you and your kids.

Focus on Your Strengths

Every family has struggles, but starting with your strengths sets a positive tone. Without this, you might slip into negativity, missing what's already working.

Spot Your Positives

Try this: Write down five things you love about:

- Your family (e.g., game nights, shared humor)
- Your home (e.g., cozy corners, big windows)
- Your neighborhood (e.g., parks, friendly neighbors)
- Your kids' school (e.g., caring teachers, art programs)
- Your job (e.g., flexibility, purpose)
- Your lifestyle (e.g., weekend hikes, quiet evenings)
- Your social network (e.g., supportive friends, fun cousins)

Share these at dinner or bedtime. Say, "I'm grateful for our movie nights; they make me smile." This builds positivity and inspires your kids to notice the good stuff too. A 2024 study in *Emotion* reinforces this idea, finding that regular gratitude practice increases parental well-being.

> **The Power of Gratitude**
> Research backs gratitude's impact. A 2023 study in Antalya, Turkey, showed that parents who journaled gratitude for fourteen days felt less stressed than a control group. Gratitude lifts your mood, health, and resilience, and spreads positivity to your kids.

Build on Strengths

Once you spot your strengths, lean into them. Love family dinners? Make them a ritual. Live near trails? Plan weekly walks. If your kid excels at art, carve out time for it. This creates a cycle of confidence, preparing you and your kids to face challenges with optimism. Acknowledging struggles is key, but dwelling on negatives can cloud your resilience. Gratitude keeps you grounded, benefiting both you and your family.

Escape the Comparison Trap

It's easy to compare your kids to others: crawling sooner, acing tests, starring in sports. You might also measure yourself against other parents: fitter, richer, happier. A little comparison is fine; it flags if your child needs support or inspires lifestyle goals. But the trap comes when you obsess, cherry-picking others' highlights and ignoring their struggles.

Social media fuels this, showing curated lives that seem perfect. Spoiler: Nobody's life is flawless. A 2023 study in the *Journal of Child and Family Studies* confirmed that excessive comparison on social platforms increases parental stress. Accepting others' imperfections fosters self-compassion, letting you see peers as inspiration, not competition. This mindset frees you to parent authentically, boosting resilience for you and your kids.

> **Rachel and Sam's Story: Prioritizing What Matters**
> Rachel and Sam, parents to Sophie (ten) and Lucas (seven), felt swamped in their busy community. Neighbors posted about elite sports, top grades, and lavish trips, making Rachel and Sam feel behind. Sam, who'd struggled with FOMO since his teens, pushed Sophie and Lucas into every activity, stressing everyone out. Rachel felt the community's expectations weighing her down.

Refocusing on Strengths
Therapy helped them cut through the noise. They listed their family's strengths: Sophie's creativity, Lucas's love for nature, their shared humor. They dropped some sports for Sophie, enrolling her in a performing arts club, where she thrived. Lucas joined a wilderness club with friends, sparking his confidence.

Family Joy
The family started art nights and nature weekends, even inviting neighbors. By focusing on their unique strengths, Rachel and Sam found peace, parenting with pride instead of pressure. Their kids grew happier, and the family's resilience soared. Parents can escape comparison by celebrating what makes their family special, inspiring kids to do the same.

Create a Thriving Family Environment

Your home shapes your family's resilience. It's not about perfection—every family has chaos—but about tailoring your space to your kids' needs.

Understand Your Kids' Needs

Kids vary. Some need high-energy outlets, like a backyard trampoline. Others crave calm, like a quiet reading nook. Notice what motivates your kids, what distracts them, and what builds their confidence. For example, a child with ADHD might need structured routines, while a shy kid benefits from social playdates. Journal these observations: "Mia focuses better with music off," or "Liam shines when praised." This self-awareness helps you tweak your home, especially for kids with learning or social needs.

Build a Supportive Space

Try these:

- **Balance activity and rest**: Mix active play (e.g., soccer) with downtime (e.g., puzzles). A 2021 study in *Pediatrics* found balanced schedules reduce stress in kids.
- **Encourage strengths**: If your kid loves music, set up a practice corner. If they're social, host game nights with friends.
- **Foster positivity**: Praise effort ("You worked hard on that drawing!") and share gratitude at meals. This builds confidence and resilience.

These tweaks create a home where everyone feels valued, strengthening your family's ability to handle challenges.

> **Jack and Amy's Story: Tailored Environments**
> Siblings Jack and Amy, each with two kids, parent differently despite shared roots. Jack, a stay-at-home dad, keeps a calm, structured home for his routine-loving kids, focusing on crafts and books. Amy, a single mom, runs a lively household for her social kids, packed with sports and community events.
>
> **Embracing Differences**
> Early on, they compared approaches, feeling inadequate. Therapy helped them value their unique

styles. Jack's quiet home suited his kids' need for focus; Amy's bustle matched her kids' energy. On joint vacations, their kids adapted, but both parents saw their home setups were right.

Family Fit
Jack and Amy's tailored environments boosted their kids' confidence and their own resilience. Parents can create thriving homes by matching their space to their family's needs, fostering growth for all.

Live Authentically

Authenticity means living true to your values, emotions, and needs. It's rooted in:

- **Self-awareness**: Knowing your thoughts, feelings, and values.
- **Self-acceptance**: Embracing your strengths and flaws.
- **Integrity**: Aligning actions with beliefs.

In parenting, authenticity is tricky; you balance your needs with those of your kids. But honoring yourself sets a powerful example.

Be True to You

Reflect on what matters to you. Love nature? Hike with your kids. Value honesty? Share your feelings openly. If you're forcing a lifestyle, like intense workouts that drain you, pause. Choose habits that fit your life. This authenticity builds confidence, helping you parent with resilience and show kids it's okay to be themselves.

Ade's Story: Fitness Her Way
Ade, a mom of two and a software developer, chased gym routines like her "fit" friends, but they never stuck. She felt guilty and lost confidence.

Finding Her Fit
A wellness coach helped Ade ditch the gym for ten-minute yoga sessions twice weekly. For cardio, she played tag or danced with her kids after school pickup. Her kids cheered her on, loving the fun.

Modeling Authenticity
Ade's realistic fitness boosted her energy and resilience. Her kids saw her prioritize health authentically, inspiring them to try new activities. Parents can live authentically by choosing habits that align with their life, modeling resilience for kids.

Lila's Story: Social Media Balance
Lila, mom to twelve-year-old Emma, scrolled Instagram, envying others' vacations and perfect homes. She pushed Emma into dance classes to "keep up," but Emma was miserable.

Redefining Success
Lila journaled her values, family time, and creativity, and cut social media time. She let Emma switch to art classes, where she shone. They started family paint nights, focusing on joy, not competition.

Authentic Joy
Lila's shift eased family tension, and Emma's confidence grew. Lila's authenticity strengthened their resilience. Parents can avoid comparison traps

Model Vulnerability

Sharing your struggles—work stress, past failures—normalizes imperfection for your kids. It says, "It's okay to mess up." This builds trust and resilience, letting them express their own challenges.

> **Jenna's Story: Connecting with Colin**
> Jenna, a single mom, noticed her thirteen-year-old, Colin, withdrawing, skipping hangouts, and snapping often. She assumed it was teen moodiness, but he showed signs of anxiety, which worried her.
>
> **Opening Up**
> Jenna, used to seeming "strong," realized her guardedness might block Colin. She carved out talk time, listening without fixing. Sharing her own school struggles and work stress, she said, "I get how hard it feels sometimes." Colin opened up about school pressure and friend drama.
>
> **Building Trust**
> Jenna's empathy—"That sounds tough; I've felt that too"—made Colin feel safe. They brainstormed coping strategies, like journaling. Their honest talks strengthened their bond, boosting Colin's resilience and Jenna's confidence. Parents can foster authenticity by sharing vulnerabilities, helping kids navigate challenges.

Authenticity Fuels Resilience

Authenticity and resilience go hand in hand. Self-awareness helps you know your family's strengths. Self-acceptance lets you embrace imperfections. Integrity aligns your parenting with your values. Parenting reshapes you, offering chances to redefine who you are. By living authentically, you build trust, show kids it's okay to be themselves, and create a resilient family ready for life's ups and downs.

How can you maximize your family's potential? The next chapter explores how focusing on strengths and intentional preparation can build both resilience and growth.

CHAPTER 9

Putting Resilience into Practice

Athletes know preparation is everything. Hours of training, conditioning, and strategy lay the groundwork for success. But the real test comes in competition, where they apply their skills and learn from the outcome, win or lose. Parenting isn't a sport or a contest, but it demands that same grit: resilience. As a psychologist, I've seen athletes sharpen traits that help them thrive under pressure. Those traits translate directly to parenting, equipping them to handle the chaos of family life with confidence and connection. In this chapter, I'll draw on my work with athletes to show how building resilient traits, living a resilient lifestyle, and putting resilience into practice can make you a stronger parent.

The Traits of a Resilient Parent

You've explored resilience strategies and stories of parents who've embraced them. Now, let's make it personal: Are you a resilient parent? It's a tough question, and most of us hesitate to answer. We see strengths in ourselves but also areas to grow. This is completely normal and expected. To help, let's revisit the core traits of resilient parenting from earlier chapters. Rate yourself out of ten for each, no overthinking. For a fresh perspective, ask a partner or friend for their input.

- **Flexibility**: Adapt to your kids' evolving needs and embrace new approaches.
- **Stress and emotional regulation**: Stay calm and patient, even in high-pressure moments.
- **Self-awareness**: Embrace your family's unique context, free from unhealthy comparisons.
- **Problem-solving**: Turn challenges into growth opportunities for you and your kids.
- **Social support**: Build and rely on relationships with family, friends, or community.
- **Self-care**: Prioritize your physical health, mental well-being, and personal passions.
- **Resilient mindset**: Stay positive, seeing possibilities beyond obstacles.
- **Emotional intelligence**: Tune into your emotions and your kids', fostering empathy.
- **Effective communication**: Listen actively and explain your choices clearly.
- **Boundaries and independence**: Set healthy limits while encouraging your kids' autonomy.

No parent masters every trait. That's not the point. This book is about progress, not perfection, building resilience in your own way and in your own time. These traits are your tools, and the self-scoring exercise helps you identify where you shine and where you can grow. It's like an athlete reviewing game footage: You celebrate strengths and target weaknesses for improvement.

Lessons from Athletes

My work with athletes offers powerful insights for parenting. Their strategies for peak performance translate seamlessly to building resilience at home. Let's dive into three key lessons, packed with practical steps and real stories.

1. Play to Strengths, Work on Weaknesses

Athletes excel by leveraging strengths while tackling weaknesses. A sprinter who starts fast but fades late gains more from endurance drills than from perfecting their launch. Strengths build confidence; weaknesses fuel growth. Parenting works the same way. Look at the traits above; where do you stand out? Maybe you're great at connecting with your kids but struggle with stress. That's your signal to focus there.

Accepting weaknesses isn't about self-doubt. Research shows that when we acknowledge gaps without judgment, we're more likely to improve. If emotional regulation is a challenge, try small steps like five minutes of deep breathing or journaling daily frustrations. These efforts strengthen you and show your kids it's okay to work on imperfections. For example, one parent I coached noticed they snapped at their kids during hectic mornings. By practicing mindfulness, pausing for three deep breaths before reacting, they became calmer, and their kids responded with less tension, creating a smoother start to the day.

2. A Resilient Lifestyle Maximizes Potential

Resilience thrives on a lifestyle that supports your best self. Parenting is demanding, but it's easier with energy, clarity, and confidence. There's no one-size-fits-all plan; your lifestyle must reflect your values and context. Ask yourself:

- **Physical well-being**: Do I prioritize sleep, nutrition, exercise, or stress relief?
- **Emotional well-being**: Do I make time for mindfulness, hobbies, or reflection?
- **Routine**: Does my schedule align with my family's needs?
- **Work–life balance**: Can I separate work stress from home life?
- **Reflection**: Do I check in with my needs and my kids' needs?
- **Relationships**: Do I spend quality time with my kids and communicate with empathy?
- **Support network**: Do I connect with and lean on others regularly?

One parent I worked with, a former marathon runner, felt drained after stopping running post-kids. Work stress spilled into family life, and their routine was chaotic. They set a goal to run another marathon, starting with short jogs during school hours. Over a year, they built up to the full distance, finishing close to their personal best. When I asked about the race, they said the finish line was great, but the real transformation happened during training. Running restored their physical and emotional health, gave them a structured routine, and provided quiet moments to reflect on work and family separately. Family dinners became more relaxed, and their kids noticed a happier, more present parent. This parent's story shows that a resilient lifestyle, whether through running, painting, or meditation, fuels your parenting and models balance for your kids.

Another parent, a busy dad named Mark, struggled with work–life balance. His long hours left him short-tempered at home. He started scheduling fifteen-minute walks after work to decompress, leaving his phone behind. Those walks became a ritual to shift from work to family mode, helping him engage with his kids more patiently. His daughter even joined him sometimes, turning walks into bonding moments. Small changes like these build a lifestyle that supports resilience for you and your family.

3. Moments Make Us

Athletes train for months, but their legacy is built in key moments, races, games, or clutch plays. Parents face similar defining moments daily. Challenges are inevitable, but resilient parents tackle them with emotional intelligence, problem-solving, and patience.

They embrace mistakes as part of growth, teaching their kids to do the same. By facing challenges head-on, you show your kids how to navigate life's ups and downs.

The stories below highlight parents who turned tough moments into opportunities, modeling resilience for their children.

> **Helen and Emma's Story — Overcoming Injury:** Emma, a dedicated rower since age twelve, faced a major setback in her senior year of high school. A shoulder injury required surgery and months of physical therapy, leaving her uncertain about competing again. Her single mom, Helen, stepped up as her anchor. Raising Emma alone, Helen drew on resilience to support them both. She explained the surgery and recovery process clearly, keeping Emma focused on the end goal. To ease the frustration of setbacks, Helen encouraged Emma to explore new passions, like sketching landscapes and volunteering at her rowing club, giving her purpose beyond the sport.
>
> Helen leaned on their community—teachers, classmates, and rowing peers—for encouragement. She also brought me in for professional support, knowing Emma needed extra guidance. Helen drove her to appointments, guided her through exercises, and celebrated small wins, like regaining arm mobility. She shared her own story of overcoming a tough career layoff, showing Emma that resilience means pushing forward despite fear. Those conversations deepened their bond, turning recovery into a shared journey.
>
> Seven months post-injury, Emma competed in a major race. Her team's victory sparked cheers from a supportive crowd, many there for Emma. The journey wasn't easy, but it brought Helen and Emma closer. Helen's steady presence taught Emma that resilience is about growing through adversity, a lesson that shaped her approach to life beyond rowing.

> **Anna and Caleb's Story — Bouncing Back from Surgery:** Caleb, a talented teen golfer, dreamed of competing at the highest level. A congenital heart condition requiring surgery threatened that goal. His mom, Anna, had always championed his passion, especially after her divorce, when golf became Caleb's refuge. Determined to help him return to the course, Anna drew on her own resilience, forged through single parenthood.
>
> Anna encouraged Caleb to use his recovery time wisely, studying golf strategies and mental techniques. When he returned to play, his drives were weaker, frustrating him. Anna reminded him to focus on his strength, his precise short game, while rebuilding power gradually. She shared how she rebuilt confidence post-divorce by focusing on what she could control, like her routine and emotional intelligence. This gave Caleb perspective: Progress was the goal, not perfection.
>
> Anna connected Caleb with a local golf coach for extra support and arranged family game nights to keep his spirits high. When Caleb competed again, his joy in playing, not just winning, returned. Anna's support showed him that resilience means adapting and finding strength in tough moments. Their journey deepened their trust, making Caleb feel supported and Anna more confident as a parent.

These stories show resilience in action. Helen and Anna faced personal struggles but used flexibility, emotional intelligence, and support networks to guide their kids through challenges. Their examples taught Emma and Caleb that obstacles are opportunities to grow, not barriers. By modeling resilience, they equipped their kids with a mindset to face life's challenges with courage.

Building Resilience, Moment by Moment

Resilience isn't a single trait; it's built through practice. Whether you're managing stress, leaning on others, or embracing your family's unique path, every step strengthens you. Like athletes, parents shine in the moments that test them. By tackling challenges with empathy and problem-solving, you grow stronger and show your kids how to do the same. Resilience is forged in these moments, one choice at a time.

What can you do when a challenge feels too big to handle alone? The next chapter explores when and how to seek professional support and why it can be a powerful step toward resilience.

CHAPTER 10

Why, How, and When to Seek Help

Resilience doesn't mean going it alone. It's about tapping into resources, books, friends, or family. Sometimes, the smartest move is seeking professional help. Nearly half of Americans see a therapist, coach, or counselor at some point, yet stigma keeps many from reaching out. This chapter demystifies professional support, showing why it's a strength, when to seek it, and how to find the right fit for your family.

Why Seek Help?

Therapy isn't a sign of weakness; it shows strength, resourcefulness, and self-awareness. It sends your kids a powerful message: Asking for help is okay. Parents who seek therapy model resilience and improve their overall sense of well-being. Despite progress since I began practicing in the 1990s, stigma persists. Many people worry about judgment or think therapy's only for a crisis. It's not. Whether you're navigating stress or aiming to grow, professional support offers clarity and tools.

> **Maria's Story: Therapy's Family Impact**
> Maria's son, Daniel, struggled at school, growing withdrawn. Her husband, Fabian, had lost his job, and financial stress strained Maria's well-being. Daniel's teacher suggested counseling, but he resisted, fearing peers' opinions. Maria, proud and self-reliant, hesitated too; therapy felt like admitting failure.
>
> **Taking the Leap**
> After a heated argument with Daniel over a small issue, Maria saw her own stress mirrored in him. She contacted a school-recommended family therapist offering discounts. Sessions helped them share openly: Fabian's lost confidence, Maria's financial burden, Daniel's home worries.
>
> **Stronger Together**
> Therapy fostered empathy and support. Maria learned stress management, Daniel opened up, and Fabian regained purpose. Their bond grew, proving therapy builds resilience. Parents can model strength by seeking help, guiding kids to do the same.

When to Seek Help

There's no minimum threshold for professional support. If a challenge disrupts your or your family's life, happiness, work, or relationships, it's time. Don't wait for a crisis. Common reasons to seek professional help include:

- **Mental health struggles**: Persistent anxiety, depression, or mood changes affecting daily life.
- **Injury or illness**: Physical or mental strain from chronic conditions.
- **Life transitions**: Divorce, relocation, or grief.
- **Trauma**: Past or recent events like accidents or violence.
- **Chronic stress**: Ongoing overwhelm impacting health or parenting.
- **Developmental concerns**: Worries about a child's emotional or social growth.
- **Relationship issues**: Conflicts between parents or with kids.
- **Performance blocks**: Procrastination, fear, or low motivation.

If you're considering therapy, take it as a sign that you would benefit from it. Acting early shows commitment to thriving, not just surviving.

> **Need to Know: Emergencies:** Therapy isn't for emergencies. For immediate risks, call 911 or visit an ER. For nonemergency support, call 988 24/7 for confidential help and local resources.

Types of Support

Therapy and coaching can overlap but differ in focus. Here's a quick guide:

Type	Focus	Duration	Best For
Therapy	Mental health, emotional challenges	Short- or long-term	Anxiety, depression, trauma
Coaching	Goal-oriented, personal growth	Short-term	Parenting strategies, performance blocks

Each approach draws on various techniques, often blended for your needs. Key options include:

- **Cognitive behavioral therapy (CBT)**: Helps to identify and change negative thoughts and behaviors.
- **Psychodynamic therapy**: Explores past experiences to understand emotions.
- **Humanistic therapy**: Fosters self-growth in a supportive space.
- **Resilience therapy**: Builds coping skills and adaptability. Combines CBT and positive psychology.
- **Integrative therapy**: Tailors multiple methods to your needs, addressing mind and body.
- **Parent coaching**: Enhances parenting strategies and family dynamics.
- **Couples therapy**: Improves communication and intimacy between partners.

- **Family therapy**: Strengthens family bonds and resolves conflicts.

Javier's Story: Healing Trauma
Javier, a dad of two, faced sleepless nights after a car accident. His kids noticed his irritability, and he withdrew, fearing he was failing them.

Finding Support
Javier tried CBT with a therapist, learning to reframe anxious thoughts. He also learned coping strategies and benefited greatly from the support of his therapist.

Family Healing
Javier's calm returned, and he shared coping strategies with his kids, like breathing exercises. His openness strengthened their trust. Parents can heal personal challenges through therapy, modeling resilience for kids.

Benefits of Therapy

Therapy offers three core outcomes, transforming how you parent and live:

1. **Self-awareness**: Talking openly reveals your thoughts and emotions. Such clarity can boost decision-making and confidence.
2. **Coping skills**: Therapists teach strategies to manage stress, anxiety, or conflicts, replacing unhealthy habits with effective ones.

3. **Stronger relationships**: Therapy sharpens communication and empathy, improving family dynamics, whether through family sessions or solo work.

These benefits help you thrive, not just cope, setting a resilient example for your kids.

Lila's Story: Parenting Confidence
Lila, a mom of a defiant teen, felt overwhelmed by constant arguments. She doubted her parenting, fearing she was too strict.

Gaining Tools
Lila tried parent coaching, learning to set boundaries with empathy. Role-playing helped her communicate calmly.

Family Shift
Lila's teen responded to her new approach, reducing conflicts. Lila's confidence grew, and she modeled problem-solving for her kid. Parents can use coaching to navigate tough phases, building resilience for all.

Finding the Right Therapist

Choosing a therapist can feel daunting, but these steps make it manageable:

1. **Identify your needs**: Want help with stress, parenting, or trauma? Clarify your goals to narrow options.

2. **Check credentials**: Look for licensed therapists (e.g., LMFT, LCSW) or certified coaches. Verify via state boards or organizations like the American Psychological Association.

3. **Use directories**: Platforms like Psychology Today or GoodTherapy list professionals by specialty and location.

4. **Ask questions**: In initial calls, ask about their approach, experience, and fees. Ensure they're a good fit for your family's needs.

5. **Trust your gut**: Comfort and trust matter. If the first session feels off, try another professional.

A 2021 study in the *Journal of Consulting and Clinical Psychology* reinforces the importance of the therapeutic alliance between therapist and client. Take your time to find the right match.

Tips for Success

- Be open about your challenges; honesty fuels progress.
- Set realistic goals with your therapist, like managing stress in a month.
- Expect ups and downs; therapy takes time.
- Involve family if needed, like in Maria's case, for shared growth.

Therapy Fostering Resilience

Therapy isn't a quick fix; it's a partnership. My clients arrive with varied goals: Some seek clarity; others need urgent support. My role is to listen without judgment, offering a safe space to explore challenges. Like Maria, Javier, and Lila, you can use therapy to grow stronger, navigate crises, and model resilience for your kids. It's not about fixing flaws; it's about unlocking potential.

How can challenges become opportunities for growth? The next chapter looks at how self-reflection helps parents find clarity, meaning and possibility.

CHAPTER 11

Reflecting on Your Parenting Journey

Parenting is a unique adventure, filled with joy, challenges, and constant growth. Your relationship with your kids evolves daily—you teach them; they teach you. You strive to balance safety and structure with freedom to grow. Amid this emotional, rewarding, and sometimes daunting journey, it's natural to seek validation. You look for a way to measure your progress, but no universal standard exists. Every family faces distinct challenges, and success looks different for each child. Friends and family can offer support, reminding you you're doing great or nudging you to adjust. But true validation comes from within. Only you know your struggles, your values, and your kids' needs. Learning to validate yourself builds resilience, empowering you to parent with confidence and model strength for your children.

The Power of Self-Reflection

Self-reflection is your compass in parenting. It helps you adapt to challenges, spot areas to grow, and manage stress thoughtfully. A comprehensive review of 301 studies in *Mindfulness* (2024) showed that self-reflective parenting correlates to improved well-being for both parents and children. By looking back on your actions and emotions, you gain clarity, learn from mistakes, and celebrate wins. This chapter shows how to use self-reflection to track your progress, recognize your strengths, and validate your journey.

Here are five principles for effective self-reflection:

1. **Perfection isn't the goal**: No parent is perfect. Reflection helps you improve while embracing flaws as chances to grow.
2. **Define your own success**: Avoid comparing yourself to others. Success aligns with your values and circumstances.
3. **Parenting never stops**: It's a lifelong journey. Success means offering support at every stage, from infancy to adulthood.
4. **Learn, don't dwell**: Mistakes are lessons. Focus on how you'll apply them, not on regrets.
5. **Use what you have**: Every parent navigates unique challenges. Resilience comes from making the most of your resources.

Lila's Story: Reflecting on Growth
Lila, a mom of two teens, felt inadequate, comparing herself to "perfect" parents online. Her kids' bickering and her short temper left her discouraged.

Finding Clarity
Lila started journaling weekly, noting triggers like work stress and wins like calm family dinners. Reflecting helped her see patterns: She was patient when rested; she prioritized sleep and set boundaries with her teens.

Validating Herself
Looking back, Lila saw how far she'd come. Her teens opened up more, and conflicts dropped. Journaling showed her resilience, boosting her confidence. Parents can use reflection to validate their progress, modeling growth for kids.

Self-Reflection Equals Self-Appreciation

Reflection isn't just about fixing what's broken—it's about seeing your growth with compassion. It's easy for us as parents to focus on the hard moments: the meltdowns, the doubts, the times we didn't respond the way we hoped. But when we step away and look at the broader picture, we often find something else: quiet evidence of strength. Maybe you're more patient than you used to be. Maybe you're learning to pause instead of react. Maybe you've started to notice what your child needs beneath their behavior. Reflection helps us see that we are, in fact, growing alongside our kids. It reminds us that resilience isn't built in big moments—it's built in the small, steady steps we take each day toward becoming more present, more grounded, and more intentional in how we show up.

Journal Your Journey

Journaling helps you track experiences and emotions. Write daily or weekly, noting events, feelings, and lessons. Try prompts like:

- What went well today? (e.g., "Listened calmly to Mia's frustration.")
- What challenged me? (e.g., "Lost patience during homework.")
- What did I learn? (e.g., "I need a break when stressed.")

Digital journals, like apps or weekly emails to yourself, can include photos or voice notes, creating a rich record. One client emailed herself weekly, blending facts and feelings, like a digital scrapbook. This helped her see growth over time.

Revisit Memories

Photos spark reflection but often highlight happy moments, missing challenges. Balance this by journaling alongside photos. For example, a beach trip photo might recall joy but also a tantrum you navigated well. Reflecting on both builds a fuller picture, showing your resilience in tough moments.

> **Journaling Tip:** Set a weekly timer for ten minutes. Write one win, one challenge, and one goal. Over months, you'll see patterns and progress.

Assessing Your Resilience

Three questions guide you in measuring your resilience as a parent, focusing on you, your kids, and your relationship.

How Are You Doing?

Resilient parents prioritize self-care, health, hobbies, and emotional balance. We know that consistent self-care can reduce parental burnout. Check your emotional regulation: Do you stay calm under stress? Reflect on your life, work, social connections, health, or broader worries like finances or the world. Pinpointing stress sources (e.g., "Work deadlines make me snap") helps you address them, like setting boundaries or practicing mindfulness.

How Are Your Kids Doing?

A supportive home helps kids feel safe and express emotions in a healthy way. Notice their enthusiasm for school, friends, or hobbies. Are they resilient to setbacks? A child's overall well-being often reflects the overall dynamics at home; stress, connection, and emotional support all impact a child's level of coping. This simple question invites deeper reflection about how your child is doing and the environment shaping their growth and resilience.

How's Your Relationship with Your Child?

Strong bonds thrive on trust, communication, and respect. Kids should feel safe seeking your guidance. Share your own struggles in an age-appropriate way to normalize challenges. Even turbulent phases are normal; what matters is staying available, offering security through every challenge.

Mark's Story: Rebuilding Connection
Mark, a dad of a twelve-year-old, felt distant from his son, Liam, who was glued to video games. Mark's lectures led to arguments.

Reflecting and Adjusting
Mark journaled, realizing his frustration stemmed from long work hours. He started weekly game nights, playing Liam's games with him. He shared his own teen struggles, opening honest talks.

Stronger Bond
Liam began confiding in Mark, and their trust grew. Mark's reflection rebuilt their connection, showing Liam resilience through openness. Parents can strengthen bonds by reflecting and adapting.

Parenting Keeps Evolving

Parenting adapts to your child's stages, each with unique needs. Tailored strategies boost resilience across development by meeting children where they are, supporting their unique emotional, cognitive and social needs at each stage.

- **Infancy**: Focus on secure attachment through consistent care, cuddles, and feeding routines. Example: Respond promptly to cries to build trust.

- **Early childhood**: Support autonomy with routines and praise. Example: Let a toddler choose their shirt, reinforcing independence.

- **Middle childhood**: Guide academics and social skills while fostering independence. Example: Help with homework but encourage problem-solving.

- **Adolescence**: Respect growing autonomy with open communication. Example: Discuss peer pressure calmly, sharing your own experiences.

- **Early adulthood**: Shift to an advisory role, supporting independence. Example: Offer job search tips but let them lead.

Every parent navigates these stages differently. Some love the closeness of infancy; others thrive in the debates of adolescence. You don't need to love every phase, just adapt with empathy and resilience within your strengths and context.

Sarah's Story: Adapting to Teens
Sarah struggled with her fifteen-year-old's mood swings. She loved early childhood but found teens baffling.

Evolving Approach
Reflecting, Sarah saw she was too controlling. She tried active listening, letting her teen vent without fixing. She journaled wins, like a calm talk about school.

Resilient Shift
Their relationship warmed, and Sarah's teen sought her advice. Adapting built Sarah's confidence,

showing her teen's resilience through flexibility. Parents can evolve by reflecting on a child's needs at each stage.

Celebrate Your Wins

As I wrote this book, I reflected on my own parenting. Raising twin boys, now seventeen, was overwhelming at first: sleepless nights, endless diapers. Stepping away helped me learn to pause before reacting, lean on friends, and embrace mistakes. From stressed new mom to confident parent, I've built resilience, empathy, and patience. It's not perfect, and it never will be, but by practicing strategies to calm my mind and body and prioritize my overall wellbeing, I can show up more fully for myself and for my family.

Every parent I've worked with amazes me. Each brings unique strengths—humor, patience, creativity—to their journey. Resilient parenting doesn't dictate how to raise your kids. It equips you with tools to navigate the journey with clarity and confidence. You're more attuned to your kids, ready for challenges and modeling resilience.

What's the one moment you'll look back on that reminds you that you were exactly the parent your kids needed? The next chapter explores how parenting evolves alongside our children, and why there's no single right way to do it.

CHAPTER 12

Living the Keys to Resilient Parenting

Resilient parenting is not a theory for me. It is the path I have walked—as a clinical psychologist, yes, but also as a mother, a wife, a daughter, and a woman who has faced her own times of uncertainty, fear, and transformation. *Step Away: The Keys to Resilient Parenting* is more than a book; it is a reflection of lived truth, forged in the messy, beautiful moments of raising twin boys, counseling families, and navigating my own story. This chapter brings that journey full circle, where the clinical and the deeply personal converge to show you, the reader, what's possible, not when life is perfect, but when you choose to engage differently with its imperfections.

Parenting from the Inside Out

Resilience begins on the inside. I learned this early, as a child grappling with a medical diagnosis that turned my world upside down. In Chapter 1, I shared how that experience, of hospital rooms, uncertainty, and finding strength in small moments, became my first teacher. It taught me that resilience isn't fixed; it's cultivated through patience, adaptation, and hope. That lesson stayed with me, a quiet compass guiding my work as a psychologist and my life as a mother.

Raising our twin boys, Ethan and Lucas, has been the greatest test of that compass. Like every parent, I've faced moments where answers eluded me: tantrums in Chapter 3, sleepless nights in Chapter 5, or the quiet fears of wondering if I was enough. But those moments also showed me that presence trumps perfection. Intention outweighs control. When we step away, from urgency, reactivity, or impossible standards, we create space for grace, for our children and ourselves.

From the Clinic to the Kitchen Table

In my practice, I've sat with hundreds of families, listening to their worries, grief, guilt, and love. I've seen how burnout erodes a parent's spirit, how isolation amplifies small failures, and how hope flickers when someone feels truly seen. The strategies in this book, introduced in Chapters 4 through 10, were born in that space between theory and practice. They came not from textbooks but from real families navigating messy, beautiful lives.

One lesson stands out: the power of stepping away. When parents give themselves permission to stop, they open the door to awareness. They hear their inner dialogue, get curious about their reactions, and find alignment between their values and actions. This isn't about overnight breakthroughs; it's about slow, steady shifts, like the family in Chapter 7 who rediscovered connection by pausing to listen rather than fix.

Letting Go: A Personal Story

There was a moment that crystallized everything for me, a quiet, ordinary moment that carried extraordinary weight.

It was a chilly November afternoon, and Ethan came home from school, his backpack slung low, his face shadowed. At ten, he was navigating the choppy waters of middle school friendships, and a misunderstanding with a friend had left him feeling rejected. He slumped onto a kitchen stool, tracing a scratch on the counter, his usual chatter replaced by silence. As a mother, my heart ached to see him so deflated. As a psychologist, my mind raced to analyze: perhaps a bruised sense of belonging, a need for social skills coaching.

Every instinct urged me to fix it. I wanted to call the teacher, email the friend's parents, or hand Ethan a script to resolve it. But I caught myself. Years of training whispered: *Listen first. Be present.* I pulled up a stool, the kitchen warm with the scent of cinnamon from breakfast's oatmeal. "Sounds like today was tough," I said softly, mirroring his tone. "Want to tell me what happened?"

He shrugged; eyes fixed on the counter. Then, slowly, he spoke about a friend who turned away, a moment that stung. I nodded, resisting the urge to offer solutions. "That sounds really hard," I said. "How do you want to handle it?" He looked up, surprised, as if he hadn't expected to be trusted with the answer. As he talked, his shoulders lifted. His voice grew steadier. He mapped out a plan, a conversation, a boundary. I sat in the discomfort, trusting his resilience, trusting my own.

That evening, as we cleared the dinner plates, Ethan hugged me, a quick, wordless squeeze. I realized this was stepping away: not checking out but trusting the process. As a psychologist, I saw the power of mirroring, helping him feel seen. As a mom, I felt the weight of letting go, believing he could find his way.

Another Lesson in Connection

Another moment, with Lucas, taught me resilience in a different light. One evening, after a chaotic day, I snapped at him over a spilled glass of juice. My voice was sharper than intended, and his face fell, eyes wide with hurt. The guilt hit like a wave. I'd spent years teaching parents to avoid reacting from stress, yet here I was, caught in my own reactivity.

I took a breath and sat beside him on the couch. "I messed up," I said. "I was frustrated, but that's not your fault. Let's try that again." His surprise softened into a small smile. We talked it through; he apologized for the spill, I for my tone. That moment wasn't about juice; it was about modeling accountability, showing him that mistakes don't define us, but repairs do. As a psychologist, I knew this taught emotional regulation. As a mom, I wanted him to see that love means owning our flaws. We laughed about the "juice incident," turning a rupture into connection.

Resilient Parenting Is an Ongoing Practice

Resilient parenting is a practice, not a checklist. Like mindfulness or therapy, it's something you live. Some days, you'll pause and respond with grace. Others, you'll yell in the car or forget every tool you've learned. That's not failure; it's being human. The shift happens when we measure ourselves not by mistakes but by our willingness to reconnect, with our children and ourselves.

As a psychologist, I know the science of resilience. As a mother, I know the weight of showing up. As someone who's faced adversity, I know the stakes. Resilient parenting meets you at that intersection, asking for presence, humility, and courage.

Why This Book Needed to Be Written

I wrote *Step Away* for parents drowning in stress, shame, and self-doubt. In Chapter 2, I shared my own early struggles as a mother, feeling the pressure to be "on" 24/7. I saw that same pressure in my clients: good, loving parents depleted by the chase for perfection. This book offers a new lens: Start with you. Your energy, your values, your nervous system. When you're grounded, everything changes: your responses, your boundaries, your child's sense of safety.

It's not magic. It's the ripple effect of resilient parenting.

What Readers Can Take with Them

If you take nothing else from this book, take these truths:

- Your well-being is the foundation of everything you build for your child.
- You are not behind. Every day is a chance to parent with intention.
- You are allowed to step away, from guilt, pressure, or hustle, to care for yourself.
- You are the model. Your children learn resilience from how you live, not what you say.

Try this: Take ten minutes to journal about a recent parenting moment. What emotions came up? What value did you want to embody? How could you "step away" next time to respond with intention? This isn't about perfection; it's about starting where you are.

The Science Is Clear, But So Is the Soul

The science of resilience is clear: Self-aware, emotionally flexible parents raise secure, independent children. But the soul of this work lives in the 3 a.m. worries, the guilt after a rough day, the fierce love that keeps you going. *Step Away* honors that soul, reminding you that you don't have to do this alone or get it right every time.

Coming Home to Ourselves

Congruence, when our internal experience matches our external actions, is gold in parenting. When you live your values, your children feel it. They sense your steadiness as safety. But many of us weren't raised with this alignment, so we learn it in real time, often while raising our kids. Parenting becomes a mirror, reflecting our wounds and inviting transformation.

Legacy Isn't What We Leave Behind; It's What We Live

Legacy isn't just about the future; it's about today. The moments—how we handle a spilled glass, apologize after a fight, or show self-compassion—shape our children's emotional blueprints. When we repair ruptures or model grace, we give them permission to be human too.

Stepping Away Is a Radical Act of Leadership

In a world of Instagram-perfect parents and overscheduled lives, stepping away is radical. It's refusing to parent from depletion. It's choosing influence over control, modeling resilience by caring for your own energy. Research shows that constant comparison spikes stress hormones, undermining calm responses. By stepping away, you reclaim clarity and courage.

As I write this, our boys, now seventeen, are in the thick of late adolescence, navigating the final stretch of high school and eyeing college on the horizon. Their new questions and challenges, from

Ethan's guarded moments to Lucas's quieter days, signal a shift not just for them but for me as a parent. Preparing for their transition to college feels like stepping into uncharted territory, demanding new tools and trust in their growing independence. What do you do when the strategies that carried you through one phase no longer fit? When your children stand at a crossroads, and you must trust them to step forward, even as your own heart trembles? I don't have all the answers, not yet. But I know this: The journey of resilient parenting is about to take us somewhere new, somewhere uncharted. And I'm ready to step into it, with open eyes and an open heart.

CHAPTER 13

Navigating the Uncharted – Resilience in Transition

As our boys navigate the final stretch of adolescence, the familiar ground of parenting feels like it's shifting beneath my feet. They're on the cusp of high school graduation, their sights set on college, bringing new questions and challenges that test the tools of pausing, listening, and stepping away, as shared in Chapters 4, 7, and 9. As a parent, I'm preparing for yet another transition: adapting to their growing independence, remaining their anchor while my role as a mother demands a delicate recalibration. This chapter is about navigating that uncharted terrain, about finding resilience when the path feels uncertain and the stakes feel higher than ever.

Managing Your Triggers

Adolescence tests not just our kids but us. Lucas's habit of ignoring repeated reminders to do chores, like leaving dishes piled in the sink, can spark my frustration. As a psychologist, I know triggers are signals, pointing to unhealed parts of ourselves. As a mom, they feel personal, like a challenge to my patience. Stepping away means noticing the physical signs—tight chest, racing thoughts—and choosing a different response.

Try this: Next time you feel triggered, pause for a moment. Notice your body; where's the tension? Take five slow breaths, as Chapter 5 suggests, and ask yourself: What's this reaction about? Is it about now, or something older? Then, choose one small action to reconnect, maybe a calm conversation about the dishes or an apology for snapping. This practice builds resilience, turning triggers into opportunities for growth.

A Moment of Trust

One evening, Ethan lingered in the kitchen, his phone glowing in his hand, a habit that's become both a lifeline and a source of tension. I wanted to ask about his day, his friends, that guarded look I'd seen weeks ago. Instead, I leaned on a lesson from Chapter 4: Create space, not pressure. I poured us chamomile tea, the steam curling in the dim light of our cozy kitchen, the clock ticking softly. "I'm here when you're ready to talk," I said, keeping my voice light, almost casual.

He nodded, eyes on his screen. I busied myself with dishes, the clink of plates filling the silence. Then, unexpectedly, he spoke. "School's weird," he said, voice low. "Everyone's changing. It's like I don't know who to trust." I paused, mirroring his words: "Sounds like things feel different, like it's hard to know who's real." Slowly, he opened up, about cliques forming, about a friend who'd betrayed his confidence. I shared a story from my teenage years, a time I felt lost in a sea of social expectations, hoping it would resonate without preaching.

As a psychologist, I recognized his need for autonomy, a hallmark of adolescent development. Studies show teens thrive when parents offer guidance without control, fostering what researchers call "scaffolded independence." As a mom, I wanted to shield him from the sting of rejection, to make his world safe again. Instead, I asked, "What feels right for you right now?" That question, rooted in trust, opened a door. He didn't have all the answers, but he started sketching a plan: a conversation with his friend, a boundary to set. Later, as he headed upstairs, he tossed a casual "Thanks, Mom" over his shoulder. It was a small victory, but in that moment, it felt like we'd crossed a bridge together.

Testing Boundaries, Testing Me

Lucas, our other son, brought a different challenge. His boundary testing—leaving dishes piled in the sink, pushing back on curfews—has a way of sparking my own reactivity. One Saturday, after he ignored a request to clean his room, I felt the familiar tightening in my chest, the urge to lecture rising. As a psychologist, I know this is normal: Teens test limits to assert independence, and our own experiences can at times intensify the impact of such moments.

Instead of escalating, I stepped outside, breathing in the crisp fall air, letting the tension ease. When I returned, I sat with Lucas at the dining table to discuss the situation. "I got frustrated earlier,"

I said. "Let's figure this out together." His surprise softened into a nod. We negotiated a chore schedule, and he even cracked a joke about my "psychologist voice." As a mom, I felt the relief of connection; as a psychologist, I saw the power of modeling accountability. That moment wasn't about a clean room; it was about showing Lucas that conflicts can lead to understanding.

The Digital Dilemma

The digital world adds another layer to this terrain. Ethan's phone scrolling, Lucas's late-night texts, these are new situations I didn't face as a young parent. Research from Chapter 8 shows that excessive screen time can increase anxiety and disrupt sleep, yet heavy-handed bans often spark rebellion. As a psychologist, I advocate for coregulation: setting boundaries collaboratively while modeling healthy tech use. As a mom, I've stumbled, arguing over screen time only to realize connection trumps control.

One night, Lucas and I made a deal: no phones at dinner, but we'd play a board game after. His eye roll gave way to laughter as we battled over Scrabble, his competitive streak lighting up the room. That ritual, inspired by Chapter 9's focus on shared moments, became a weekly tradition, a pocket of connection in a digital storm. I've since invited Ethan to join, and though he grumbles, he's started suggesting games. These moments remind me: Resilience means meeting our kids where they are, not fighting their world.

The View from the Clinic

In my practice, I see parents grappling with these same shifts. Maria, introduced in Chapter 13, felt her son becoming a stranger as he entered high school. "He shuts me out," she said, her voice heavy with worry. We worked on small connection points: asking open-ended questions, sharing a coffee without agenda. Over weeks, she noticed him opening up, sharing bits of his day. Another client, Jamal, struggled with his daughter's obsession with social media. "It's like she's addicted," he said. We explored coregulation, setting screen-time limits together, and he found that modeling his own tech boundaries, putting his phone away during meals, shifted her habits.

These stories echo my own. Maria's reconnection with her son mirrors my moments with Ethan; Jamal's boundary setting reflects my Scrabble nights with Lucas. The strategies in this book—pausing, connecting, stepping away—are universal, adaptable to the chaos of adolescence.

Managing Your Triggers

Adolescence challenges us as parents and can also challenge our kids. As a psychologist, I understand that triggers often reveal parts of ourselves that still need healing. But as a mom, they land hard, feeling like a test of my ability. Stepping away means tuning into those early signals—like a clenched chest or spiraling thoughts—and making a conscious choice to respond, not react. Try this: When you feel yourself getting triggered, step away briefly—not to avoid, but to reset. Jot down what you're feeling in a notebook or notes app. Give those emotions a name—anger, shame, fear—and consider where they might be coming from. Then return with intention. Instead of reacting, try asking a curious, open-ended question: "What's going on for you right now?" Creating space for reflection, not just reaction, can shift the dynamic and strengthen the connection. This is how resilience grows: moment by moment.

Resilience in Uncertainty

Parenting teens feels like sailing through fog: You can't see far, but you keep moving. The strategies in this book—pausing from Chapter 4, connecting from Chapter 9, grounding from Chapter 5—aren't static. They bend and stretch, adapting to new seasons. As our boys navigate adolescence, I'm learning to let go of the parent I was while embracing the one they need now. It's not about having answers; it's about staying curious, present, and trusting.

What Readers Can Take with Them

Here's what I hope you carry forward:

- Embrace change as a chance to grow alongside your teen.
- Trust their ability to navigate, even when it's scary.
- Create rituals—game nights, walks, shared coffee—to stay connected without control.
- Use your triggers as signals for reflection and repair.

Try this: This week, pick one ritual to share with your teen: a meal, a drive, a game. Keep it simple, no agenda. Ask an open question, like, "What's something you're excited about?" and listen. Notice how it feels to connect without fixing. This practice, rooted in Chapter 9, builds trust in small, powerful ways.

Adolescence is uncharted, but it's also an invitation, to deepen your resilience, adapt your tools, and trust the journey. The next chapter will show how these moments, big and small, weave a legacy that lasts.

CHAPTER 14

The Legacy of Resilience — Building a Future Together

The guarded looks and quiet moments with Ethan and Lucas, introduced in Chapter 12, didn't resolve in a single conversation. Late adolescence, as I explored in Chapter 13, is a season of flux, with our seventeen-year-old boys navigating the final stretch of high school and preparing for college. This shift demands new ways of stepping away while staying connected, as I adapt to their growing independence and my own transition as a parent. Ethan and Lucas are forging their own resilience, equipped with the tools of self-awareness and courage to face the challenges of college and beyond. As I reflect on this journey from my own childhood in Chapter 1 to the uncharted waters of parenting teens, I see a profound truth: Resilient parenting isn't just about raising our children. It's about growing ourselves, building a legacy that lives in every moment we show up with courage, presence, and love. This final chapter weaves together the lessons of this book, showing how small, intentional acts create a ripple effect that shapes our children, our families, and our futures.

A Partnership in Resilience

As our boys approach adulthood, I've reflected on how my parenting journey has evolved alongside my husband's role as a dad and partner. In their early years, he was often away for work, leaving me to navigate the daily chaos of raising twins. Those days tested my resilience, leaning on the tools of pausing and grounding from Chapters 4 and 5. Now, with him home more, we've embraced a "divide and conquer" approach, adapting with flexibility to meet our boys' needs. Whether it's splitting carpool duties, tackling tough conversations together, or carving out time for family rituals like game nights, we've learned to parent as a team. This partnership, forged through years of change, has taught us that resilient parenting thrives on collaboration, trust, and showing up for each other as much as for our kids.

A Final Story of Connection

Another moment cemented this truth. One morning, as I packed lunches, Ethan lingered in the kitchen, a rare quiet pause in his busy teenage rhythm. "Mom," he said, chopping carrots beside me, "thanks for not freaking out about my grades last week." I smiled, remembering the urge to lecture, the choice to listen instead, a lesson from Chapter 3's early struggles as a new mom. We talked about his goals—making the soccer team, maybe studying art—and his fears of falling behind. I shared a memory of my own fear of failure, the pressure I felt after my childhood diagnosis in Chapter 1 to prove I was enough.

As a psychologist, I saw this as coregulation: my calm presence helping him navigate his emotions. As a mom, it was a gift, a bridge to his future, built on trust. Later that week, I saw the ripple: Ethan helped Lucas with a math problem, patient in a way that echoed my pauses. That small act showed me legacy isn't what we leave behind; it's what we live, every day.

The Ripple Effect in Others

This ripple effect extends beyond our homes. In my practice, I've seen parents transform. Maria, from Chapter 13, once felt her son was a stranger, shutting her out as he navigated high school. By using Chapter 9's connection strategies—shared walks, open-ended questions—she rebuilt trust. "He told me about his girlfriend last week," she said, her eyes bright. Another client, Priya, struggled with her daughter's anxiety, amplified by social media comparisons. Drawing on Chapter 8's stress management tools, she started modeling self-care, taking yoga breaks, limiting her own screen time. Her daughter noticed, and their conversations deepened, shifting from tension to teamwork.

These stories mirror my own. Maria's walks echo my game nights; Priya's self-care reflects my pauses with Lucas. The principles in this book—pausing, connecting, stepping away—are universal, helping parents navigate adolescence and beyond.

A Practice for Your Legacy

Your legacy is unfolding now, in every small moment. Try this: Write a letter to your future self, five years from now. What do you hope your child has learned from you? Maybe it's how you stayed calm during a tantrum, apologized after a rough day, or listened without fixing. Reflect on one moment this week that felt aligned with your values. This exercise, inspired by Chapter 10's focus on values, helps you see your legacy taking shape.

Here's another practice: Create a resilience plan. List three challenges you face as a parent: maybe a teen's silence, a busy schedule, or your own stress. For each, write one "step away" action: a pause to breathe, a ritual to connect, a boundary to set. Review it weekly, adjusting as needed. This plan, rooted in Chapter 7's strategies, keeps you grounded in intention.

The Science and Soul of Resilience

The science is clear: Resilient parents raise resilient children. Research shows that emotional flexibility—pausing, reflecting, adapting—builds a child's ability to regulate emotions and face challenges. But the soul of this work lives in the everyday: the 3 a.m. worries, the guilt after a sharp word, the fierce love that keeps you going. *Step Away* honors that soul, reminding you that you don't have to be perfect or alone, you just have to keep showing up.

As I watch Ethan and Lucas move through adolescence, I know the journey doesn't end. New experiences will bring new questions, college applications, first heartbreaks, bigger choices. But the principles in this book, from Chapter 1's lessons of resilience to Chapter 13's navigation of change, are guideposts, flexible enough to carry you through any phase. You are the key. Your presence, your courage, your willingness to return to yourself, these are the gifts you give your child, your family, and the world.

This book is a letter to every parent who's ever questioned whether they are enough, who's felt the weight of responsibility, who's still learning to offer themselves grace. You are enough. You are growing. You are leading, one resilient moment at a time. Keep pausing, keep connecting, keep stepping away. The legacy you're building is already taking root, and it's more powerful than you know.

FURTHER READING

Introduction

American Psychological Association. (2023). *Infographic: Stress of parents compared to other adults*. [Press release].

Lund, K. (2017). *Bounce: Help your child build resilience and thrive in school*. Best Seller Publishing.

Office of the U.S. Surgeon General. (2024). *Parents under pressure: The U.S. Surgeon General's advisory on the mental health & well-being of parents*. U.S. Public Health Service.

Chapter 2

Vogel, E. A., Rose, J. P., Roberts, L. R., & Eckles, K. (2014). Social comparison, social media, and self-esteem. *Psychology of Popular Media Culture, 3*(4), 206–222.

Chapter 3

Bailey, R. (2017). Goal setting and action planning for health behavior change. *American Journal of Lifestyle Medicine, 13*(6), 615–618.

Benson, H. (1975). *The relaxation response.* William Morrow & Company.

Bögels, S. M., Hellemans, J., van Deursen, S., Romer, M., & van der Meulen, R. (2014). Mindful parenting in mental health care: Effects on parental and child psychopathology, parental stress, parenting, coparenting, and marital functioning. *Mindfulness, 5,* 536–551.

Bögels, S. M., & Restifo, K. (2013). *Mindful parenting in mental health care.* Springer.

Burgdorf, V., Szabó, M., & Abbott, M. J. (2019). The effect of mindfulness interventions for parents on parenting stress and youth psychological outcomes: A systematic review and meta-analysis. *Frontiers in Psychology, 10,* 1336.

Center for Child and Family Well-Being. (n.d.). *Cultivating mindfulness & compassion.* Retrieved June 15, 2025.

Clear, J. (2018). *Atomic habits: The life-changing million-copy #1 bestseller.* Random House.

Davidson, G., et al. (2024). Parental physical activity, parental mental health, children's physical activity, and children's mental health. *Frontiers in Psychiatry, 15,* 1405783.

Enayati, A. (2012, May 26). *A creative life is a healthy life.* CNN.

Lally, P., van Jaarsveld, C. H. M., Potts, H. W. W., & Wardle, J. (2010). How habits are formed: Modeling habit formation in the real world. *European Journal of Social Psychology, 40*(6), 998–1009.

Lipkin, N. (2023, July 11). *The importance of parental mental health when it comes to our children.* Forbes.

Northern Ireland Assembly, Committee for Culture, Arts and Leisure. (2012, December 20). *The relationship between physical activity and mental health: A summary of evidence and policy* (Research paper). Northern Ireland Assembly. (niassembly.gov.uk)

American Psychological Association. (2013, January 1). *How stress affects your health.*

Nomaguchi, K., & Milkie, M. A. (2004). Costs and rewards of children: The effects of becoming a parent on adults' lives. *Journal of Marriage and Family, 65*(2), 356–374.

Oh, V. K. S., Sarwar, A., & Pervez, N. (2022). The study of mindfulness as an intervening factor for enhanced psychological well-being in building the level of resilience. *Frontiers in Psychology, 13*, 1056834.

Potharst, E. S., Boekhorst, M. G. B. M., Cuijilits, I., van Broekhoven, K. E. M., Jacobs, A., Spek, V., Nyklíček, I., Bögels, S. M., & Pop, V. J. M. (2019). A randomized controlled trial evaluating an online mindful parenting training for mothers with elevated parental stress. *Frontiers in Psychology, 10*, 1550.

Pressman, S. D., Matthews, K. A., Cohen, S., Martire, L. M., Scheier, M. F., Baum, A., & Schulz, R. (2009). Association of enjoyable leisure activities with psychological and physical well-being. *Psychosomatic Medicine, 71*(7), 725–732.

University College London. (2010). Habit formation and behavioral change: Study on the 66-day rule. *European Journal of Social Psychology, 40*(6), 998–1009.

Yıldız, E., & Uzundağ, B. A. (2024). The role of perceived social support in mitigating the impact of parenting stress on children's effortful control. *International Journal of Behavioral Development, 48*(5), 462-466.

Zero to Three. (2022, April 29). *Mindfulness practices for families.*

Chapter 4

Buckley, C. K. (2013). *Co-parenting after divorce: Opportunities and challenges.* The Family Institute at Northwestern University.

Dweck, C. S. (2006). *Mindset: The new psychology of success.* Random House.

D'Urso, A., de Zoysa, N., Soni, A., Cogan, J., Thomas, T., & Gore, C. (2021). An online support group for parents of newly diagnosed children with type 1 diabetes. *Diabetes Care for Children & Young People, 11*(1), 14–18.

Kelly, J. B., & Emery, R. E. (2003). Children's adjustment following divorce: Risk and resilience perspectives. *Family Relations, 52*(4), 352–362.

Shapira, L. B., & Mongrain, M. (2010). The benefits of selfcompassion and optimism exercises for individuals vulnerable to depression. *The Journal of Positive Psychology, 5*(5), 377–389.

Chapter 5

Brelsford, V. L., Meints, K., Gee, N. R., & Pfeffer, K. (2017). Animal-assisted therapy in the classroom – A systematic review. *International Journal of Environmental Research and Public Health, 14*(7), 669.

Hinic, K., Kowalski, M. O., Holtzman, K., & Mobus, K. (2019). The effect of a pet therapy and comparison intervention on anxiety in hospitalized children. *Journal of Pediatric Nursing, 47*, 55–61.

Chapter 6

Bradberry, T. (2009). *Emotional intelligence 2.0.* HarperCollins.

Bradberry, T. (2023). *Emotional intelligence habits.* TalentSmart.

Garcia, C. A. (2024). *The moment that defines your life.* Savio Republic.

Meurisse, T. (2018). *Master your emotions: A practical guide to building confidence and self-discipline.* Independently published.

Noll, D. (2017). *De-escalate: How to calm an angry person in less than 90 seconds.* Atria Books.

Pascuzzo, K., Cyr, C., & Moss, E. (2013). Longitudinal association between adolescent attachment, adult romantic attachment, and emotion regulation strategies. *Attachment & Human Development, 15*(1), 83–103.

Szili, Á., Bakacs, M., & Barna, G. (2023). The emotional intelligence of today's parents: Influences on parenting style and parental competence. *Frontiers in Public Health, 11*, 1120994.

Chapter 7

Clear, J. (2018). *Atomic habits: The life-changing million-copy #1 bestseller.* Random House.

Heath, C., & Heath, D. (2010). *Switch: How to change things when change is hard.* Broadway Books.

Chapter 8

Cheavers, J., & Feldman, B. (2021). *The science and application of positive psychology.* Cambridge University Press.

Garner, A., Yogman, M., Committee on Psychosocial Aspects of Child and Family Health, Section on Developmental and Behavioral Pediatrics, & Council on Early Childhood. (2021, August). Preventing childhood toxic stress: Partnering with families and communities to promote relational health. *Pediatrics, 148*(2), e2021052582.

Nelson-Coffey, S. K., & Coffey, J. K. (2023). Gratitude improves parents' wellbeing and family functioning. *Emotion*. Advance online publication.

Glatz, T., Nilsson, I. J., & Andersson, M. A. (2023). Parents' feelings, distress, and self-efficacy in response to social comparisons on social media. *Journal of Child and Family Studies, 32*(8), 2453–2464.

NelsonCoffey, S. K., & Coffey, J. K. (2024). Gratitude improves parents' wellbeing and family functioning. *Emotion, 24*(2), 357–369.

Seligman, M. (2002). *Authentic happiness: Using the new positive psychology to realize your potential for lasting fulfillment.* Atria Books.

Seligman, M. (2013). *Flourish: A visionary new understanding of happiness and well-being.* Atria Books.

Selman, S. B., & Dilworth-Bart, J. E. (2024). Routines and child development: A systematic review. *Journal of Family Therapy, 46*(1), 112–138.

Toprak, B., & Sarı, Ç. (2023). The effects of a 2-week gratitude journaling intervention to reduce parental stress and enhance well-being: A pilot study among preschool parents. *Discover Psychology, 3*, 38.

Chapter 9

Horne, T., & Horne, M. (2020). *Mental toughness for young athletes: Eight proven 5-minute mindset exercises for kids and teens who play competitive sports.* Buggily Group Inc.

Loehr, J. (1990). *The mental game.* Penguin Books.

McCree, M. (2022). *The undefeated athlete: How to be a champion in any sport.* Victory Press.

Chapter 10

Del Re, A. C., Flückiger, C., Horvath, A. O., & Wampold, B. E. (2021). Examining therapist effects in the alliance–outcome relationship: A multilevel meta-analysis. *Journal of Consulting and Clinical Psychology, 89*(5), 371–388.

Gillihan, S. J. (2016). *Retrain your brain: Cognitive behavioral therapy in 7 weeks: A workbook for managing depression and anxiety.* Althea Press.

Gillihan, S. J. (2018). *Cognitive behavioral therapy made simple: 10 strategies for managing anxiety, depression, anger, panic, and worry.* Althea Press.

Hayes, S. (2005). *Get out of your mind & into your life: The new acceptance and commitment therapy.* New Harbinger Press.

Suzuki, W. (2021). *Good anxiety: Harnessing the power of the most misunderstood emotion.* Simon and Schuster.

Chapter 11

Huynh, T., Kerr, M. L., Kim, C. N., Fourianalistyawati, E., YaRong Chang, V., & Duncan, L. G. (2024). Parental reflective capacities: A scoping review of mindful parenting and parental reflective functioning. *Mindfulness, 15*(7), 1531–1602.

Post, G. (2024). Resilient parents; resilient kids: How parental selfawareness is critical to helping smart kids thrive. *Gifted Education International.*

Chapter 14

Lathren, C. R., Bluth, K., & Zvara, B. (2020). Parent selfcompassion and supportive responses to a child's difficult emotion: An intergenerational theoretical model rooted in attachment. *Journal of Family Theory & Review, 12*(3), 368–381.

www.ingramcontent.com/pod-product-compliance
Lightning Source LLC
Chambersburg PA
CBHW020341010526
44119CB00048B/552